2 # next pages →

Y0-BZB-355

ALLY
AP
TATES

1996

MAR

MAP EXPLANATION

PAVED ROADS	
IMPROVED ROADS	THRU-ROUTES
GRADED ROADS	
DIRT OR POOR ROADS	
PAVED ROADS	
IMPROVED AND GRADED ROADS	SECONDARY OR MAIN CONNECTING ROADS
DIRT OR POOR ROADS	

■10 NATIONAL PARKS
●12 NATIONAL MONUMENTS
(FOR REFERENCE NUMBERS SEE INDEX)

From Sea to Sea
In a Model T

The true story of a trip taken in 1931 by two 19-year-olds from San Francisco to New York and back in a 1921 "Tin Lizzie" called Mike

By Yvonne Ellingson

Published by Fred Pruett
2928 Pearl St.
Boulder, CO   80301

All photos in this book not otherwise identified are from the collection of Brian (Dib) Fewer. Most of them were taken by him with a "box Brownie," a simple camera common in the 1930s.

Dedicated to the memory of all Model T Fords,
wherever they may be.

It was staggering to consider what the Model T was to lead to in both industry and folkways. It certainly wove the first network of paved highways, subsequently the parkway, and then freeway and the interstate. Beginning in the early 1920's people who had never taken a holiday beyond the nearest lake or mountain could now explore the South, New England, even the West, and in time the whole horizon of the United States.

— Alistair Cooke's America

ACKNOWLEDGMENTS

Aside from texts mentioned throughout the book, a special thanks to the following resources for adding facts and new dimensions to *From Sea to Sea in a Model T*.

To Brian Fewer for allowing his scribbled journal and letters to be quoted as recorded in 1931, though written in haste without benefit of a dictionary and without knowing his grammar and spelling would be exposed to public view one day.

The California State Automobile Association (CSAA) Library.

The *San Francisco Chronicle* (various editions), August through October 1931.

The *Christian Science Monitor* (various editions), August through October, 1931.

The Federal Writer's Projects State Guides from the 1930s, including California, Colorado, Illinois, Ohio, Florida, New Jersey, New York, New Mexico, and any others I could find at the San Francisco Public Library.

Verse by the Side of the Road by Frank Ransome, Jr., Stephen Greene Press, Brattleboro, Vermont, 1965, 1972.

Autos Across America, A Bibliography of Transcontinental Automobile Travel: 1903-1940 by Carey S. Bliss, Dawson's Book Shop, Los Angeles, 1972.

TABLE OF CONTENTS

INTRODUCTION

New York or Bust

This year many thousands of tourists will run on the ragged edge through trying to keep up the speed standards set by the latest cars. A car designed to operate normally at thirty-five may be traveling beyond its braking capacity if forced to keep pace with the forty-five and fifty-mile gait of the more recent products.

— *San Francisco Chronicle*, August 2, 1931

It was June 1931, and two young men, Dib Fewer and Tod Snedeker, were headed north toward San Francisco in a 1921 Model T coupe called Mike. Behind them, firmly attached to Mike's rear end with a rope, was Tod's useless 1928 Essex sedan.

Mike was doing okay, despite the rather weighty problem of having to tow the heavy sedan. The Essex, although seven years younger than the Model T, had thrown a timing chain and broken down driving back from a Sunday picnic at Searsville Lake, south of San Francisco, the day before. Dib and Tod abandoned it overnight alongside the two-lane highway and hitched a ride back to the city. That meant both men had to take this Monday off work to come down with Mike to retrieve the Essex, and that the Sunday picnic had been pretty much ruined. The T had never done such an inconsiderate thing as break down . . . especially on a Sunday.

Mike was a hand-me-down, a throw-away car given to Dib by a neighbor who didn't know how to fix a Model T. For four years, all through high school and beyond, it had been as faithful as a horse, and a lot more serviceable.

Now Mike was once again pulling them out of a jam, and Dib wondered how much longer the Lizzie would be able to do that. How many miles had Mike covered since rolling off that assembly line in 1921? Without a mileage meter, it was impossible to tell, but the car had been well used.

More to the point, how many miles did the old flivver have left before some major flaw, some final unfixable problem, would put it off the road for good?

Dib thought Mike could do just about anything, probably make it all the way across country and back, if they wanted it to. Tod was doubtful. That was a long trip. Mike might make it, might not, too. It would be fun, though, driving over the Rockies, through Detroit to see Highland Park maybe, and all the way back to New York City. If they did make it, they could drive Mike from one end of Broadway to the other, right through all those bright lights they'd heard about.

Tod was riding in the Essex and Dib was driving the Model T. Every time they stopped to check things out, Dib came up with another reason the trip would be a darby idea. It took several stops and fast talking to convince Tod, but by the time they parked the Essex safely in front of Tod's house on 40th Avenue in San Francisco, it was decided. They would pool their money and start out for New York City as soon as possible, by midsummer if they could swing it. Mike was going to take them all the way to Broadway, and back again . . . or die trying.

The idea was crazy. New York was a lot farther away from San Francisco in 1931 than it became later on in the century, when

roads and cars improved. It was especially distant in a ten-year-old "heap" that had, despite Dib's faith, very little chance of lasting all the way across the continent — let alone back again. But Dib and Tod were just nineteen, a year out of high school, and nothing seemed really insurmountable: not the fact that both of them would have to leave jobs when a job was almost impossible to come by; not the fact that the United States was in the Great Depression; and not the fact that Tod's folks, particularly his mother, would probably never forgive him if he insisted on making the trip.

Tod had never been farther away from San Francisco than a fishing trip with his dad one summer to Auburn in northern California. He was shy, hardworking, and loved to play football on weekends with the Richmond Rattlers, their neighborhood team. He worked with his father at the California

This is a company photo of a factory new 1921 Ford Coupe, identical to Mike in year and style.
From the collections of the Henry Ford Museum and Greenfield Village.

Simplicity itself, the Model T had a ten-gallon gas can under the seat. What wound up on this basic chassis depended on what the new owner wanted to order . . . or add, after he got it home.
From an original Ford promotional booklet, courtesy of Polyprints Publishing Company.

Ink Company in the East Bay, taking the ferry every morning from San Francisco to Oakland. He probably would have been content to keep doing that, but the one thing he loved more than football was cars. Mike was a challenge to him. The Model T ran well, very well, but just how far could it go?

Dib loved football too, but was always ready for adventure. Husky and athletic, like Tod, he got a job right out of high school as an ordinary seaman on a tanker, hoping to see something of the world. As it turned out, for $65 a month and backbreaking work as a "wiper," he mostly saw the perpetually hot, noisy engine room. Trying to coax Mike across the continent was bound to be a more exciting adventure than that.

Cross-country travel was still, in 1931, quite an adventure. Although not brand new, auto travel was nonetheless very much in the early stages. Journeys had been written about in magazines and books, cross-country races had been run, prizes given, but it was to be a long while before either the roads or the cars turned cross-country travel into an air-conditioned pleasure trip, especially if you didn't have very much money. And in 1931, few people had very much extra money. Even fewer had the nerve to start out in a car as old as Mike was for a "tour," as it was called. That was pretty much left to a few newer and better-heeled autos than Mike. Roads were rough, very rough, and a car got old pretty fast. During the prosperous twenties when a car wore out, a family would just buy a new one. But by 1931, after the 1929 stock market crash, families were not so prosperous and couldn't buy as many new cars. Old ones, like Mike, were kept longer. An automobile usually lasted no more than five years, and any car that had made it that far and gone any distance away from the paved city streets had already been bumped around plenty. Gravel and dirt roads were abundant, and when a road was "graveled" that didn't necessarily mean it had an even layer of gravel on top. It might mean a lot of giant stones intermingled with smaller ones, as well as deep ruts worn where other cars had gone before.

Now although the Model T had been specifically designed to maneuver on the horse trails and dirt farm roads available in 1908 and was more than capable of handling

1931 gravel and ruts, it certainly wasn't engineered to live forever (although that idea might have appealed to Henry Ford) or to make transcontinental tours at the ripe old age of ten.

But Dib and Tod were not thinking about the practicalities of touring, or even of Henry Ford. Motorcars were an intimate and important part of their youth. Where "motoring" had once been something only the well-to-do were able to manage, by the twenties even working class folks could afford some kind of motorized wheels. The Detroit assembly lines had seen to that, by producing cars fast and cheap. Mike probably cost his first owner in 1921 about $600. In 1931 you could buy a running 1920 or 1921 Model T for about $20 or $25 through an ad in the classified section of the *San Francisco Chronicle*. And if you were lucky enough to have a neighbor who didn't know how to fix one, you might even be given one that didn't run, absolutely free, like Dib was.

Most young men, with the exception of Dib's neighbor, could fix a Model T by themselves. It was commonly said that all you needed was a screwdriver, pliers, and some baling wire to keep a Model T going. The manuals that accompanied the original Lizzies presumed that the owner would not only be piloting the car, but in all probability maintaining it as well. It had been designed to be simple, inexpensive, and fix-able. Dib and Tod understood Mike inside and out. They had to, to keep it running.

Neither one of their fathers ever knew how to drive a car, but the boys knew. They had grown up in and around the automobile, reaching their adolescence just about the same time the automobile was going through its adolescence. They were Everyman now, and it was an age when Everyman could move personal machines from one place to another faster than they ever had before. Paradoxically, it was also an era when the failing economy was, almost daily, closing down the very freedom the auto had opened up. Dib and Tod didn't know why, really, the idea of heading out with Mike had so much appeal. The spirit of adventure in their fathers and grandfathers had carried them all the way west to the Pacific Ocean. Our young heroes could go no farther. There were no new frontiers, no new lands to explore and discover. But there were untraveled roads and exciting places their families had left behind. Like young men of any era, they were curious about places they had heard about, but even more apropos to the age they were born into, they were curious to see how far they could coax their own private machine, their aging Model T, into going before it reached the end of its road.

And that's what they did.

CHAPTER ONE

A Tin Lizzie Called Mike

Mike was a good car, a beautiful car. It started out after all its defeats, you might say. It was second hand when my neighbor got it, and when he cracked it up and gave it to us, third or fourth hand. Mike was ten years old. It doesn't sound old, but in those days the roads were bum . . . Nobody knew about 100,000 miles in those days for a car, so we wanted to see how far it would go .

—Dib Fewer

The car Dib and Tod had decided to take cross country and back had rolled off the assembly line at a Ford factory in 1921, one of 15,000,000 Model T's assembled from 1908 to 1927. It was a two-seater coupe, black, of course, because that's what all Model T's were painted from 1913 to 1925. It had three foot pedals, a handbrake both to stop it from rolling down hills and to release it into high gear when appropriate, and a crank to get it started.

Six years later, in 1927, the Lizzie came to Brian Fewer, better known as Dib, then an avid football player of sixteen attending Polytechnic High School in San Francisco. It was parked in Pinky Robinson's garage, down the street from Dib, and hadn't been on the road since the year before when it tipped over onto its side (a common Model T trick) at Geary and Divisadero streets, breaking Pinky's arm ("He must have had it

out the window"), crumpling the running boards and fenders, and smashing the side windows.

Pinky had just parked his Model T in the garage after that, every once in a while attempting to get it to run again, but without much success. Once he adjusted the valves even though he couldn't start the engine, something that not only showed how little he knew about his T, but did yet more damage to the already unstartable machine. Pinky told Dib that if he thought he could get the old heap going again, why didn't he just go ahead and take it. His folks were getting tired of having it take up space in the garage, anyway.

Dib was delighted. He was convinced he could get it running again, because with the help of his older brother he had already put one Model T back together. That had been two years before, when he was fourteen, the legal driving age in California. He had paid $15 for a beat-up 1914 Model T that was in far from top-notch condition.

Pinky's 1921 Model T was in sorrier shape than the 1914 car had been in. The fenders were almost totally disengaged from the body, all the tires were flat, and of course the engine hadn't been started for almost a year.

This would have been sometime in the autumn of 1927 in the Richmond District of San Francisco. Dib and Pinky rolled the old car on its flat tires to Dib's front yard on 26th Avenue. When Dib and his brother took a close look inside, they discovered that a later engine had been dropped into the original body, probably about a 1924 model, and that the rods, bearings, and crankshaft were all in good shape. Because Pinky had filed the valve stems without first warming up the engine so the metal could expand, there were fair-sized gaps between the valves and the cam.

Luckily, because Ford had produced Model T's for so many years, repair kits had been developed for just about everything that could possibly go wrong with them. For a few cents Dib got a kit that included special caps and washers to adjust gaps on valve stems, and he made sure the engine was heated up when he put them on. Then he and his brothers put in new spark plugs, patched the tires, tied up the fenders with wire cable, dusted off the body, turned the crank . . . and it started.

By the time the Fewer family moved to 41st Avenue in 1929, the car had become a cherished member of the family. It had been used to go to Polytechnic High School daily and carried the family regularly back and forth to the Russian River, a round trip of 140 miles or more. With the help of Tod Snedeker, who lived on 40th Avenue and just happened to be a natural-born mechanic (and a former Model T owner himself), it was kept in A-1 running condition.

Mike had pretty much lost all personality during that lethargic year in Pinky's garage. This was soon remedied, however. First, because the car was attending high school, along with Dib, the trim got painted red to make it red and black, Poly's school colors. Then it got fitted with some things that weren't exactly necessities – a resounding example being a spark plug whistle. The whistle fit between the spark plug and engine head, and when Dib pulled a string that ran through the firewall into the cab, the compression under the plug blew the whistle, producing a high whine that was a real attention getter. The faster the engine ran, the louder the whistle could blow. This wasn't particularly good for the motor, because one cylinder was momentarily partially eliminated, but it certainly got the girls to turn around.

In the early days of driving, members of the Tin Can Tourists' Association tied tin cans to their radiator caps to identify themselves. Since those days, the Model T had been dubbed a Tin Lizzie, and Tin Lizzies were just naturally presumed — at least in the majority of the cases — to be ladies. Dib might have chosen an appropriately feminine name for his Lizzie, but as is sometimes the case with names, he didn't have much choice: the name got chosen for him.

His friend Charlie Weaver owned a Model T coupe of approximately the same vintage and almost identical to Dib's. He painted the trim red, too, in honor of Poly, and he and Dib would sometimes arrive at school just a few seconds after one another. First one Model T coupe with red trim would drive down Frederick Street in front of the school, and then, seconds later, another black Model T coupe with red trim would appear. They looked so similar, it really had their friends scratching their heads, wondering how a Model T could get around the block so fast. It seemed not only fitting and proper, but inevitable that everyone started calling Charlie's car "Ike" and Dib's car "Mike" after two popular comic characters of the day from a Rube Goldberg strip called "Boob McNutt."

Mike and Ike were only two of those 15,000,000 Model T's assembled by Ford between 1908 and 1927 that looked very much alike. Many Model T owners "customized" their cars much as Dib did with Mike, painting the trim and sometimes the whole car a favorite color.

In the almost twenty years they were produced, Model T's went through a lot of minor improvements and refinements, but fundamentally remained the same design, a basic car designed clearly and simply to do one thing: transport people. No matter how you dressed them up, they just weren't fancy. Mike was no exception.

The Ford had a crank in the front to kick it into life. The only gauges on the dashboard were an ammeter to show whether or not the generator was working and an oil-pressure gauge. There was no speedometer, no temperature or gas gauge, and nothing to show how many miles the car had traveled since first being assembled. It was even difficult to tell the exact year of assembly, because changes on the Model T were so gradual and sometimes well spaced you couldn't identify them. The coupe was the economy style, although every imaginable kind of extra could be purchased for it and all the other styles, from the four-seater Touring T to the sporty two-seater Roadster T. An entire industry had grown up accessorizing the Model T's, supplying everything from completely new bodies to practically new engines. And everything could be purchased to fit, precisely (or almost), any one of the styles.

The Richmond Rattlers, Dib and Tod's neighborhood team, played football most weekends during the season, and did pretty well, it seems.

Dib was content to make his own modifications on Mike. Most of the time, for example, he didn't have to turn the crank to get the Lizzie going. He just took advantage of the many hills in San Francisco. A slight incline was all he needed to roll to a lurching start. Mike would be parked with the front end pointed downhill, the wheels banked against the curb. With one foot holding the left pedal halfway down in neutral, Dib would release the hand brake, turn the wheels away from the curb, and let the car roll out. Mike would kick over from the momentum when the pedal was let out into high gear.

If that sounds complicated it's understandable. Driving Mike was never a passive activity. There were three pedals on the floorboard under the steering column. The hand brake was on the far left, a long lever that came straight up from the boards. Pushed all the way forward it put the car in high gear. Pulled all the way back it put the transmission in neutral and applied "emergency" brakes to the rear wheels (Model T handbrakes were notoriously undependable, which makes sense given this duality of purpose). When Dib cranked the motor to a start it was necessary that the parking-brake lever on the left be all the way back, the transmission thus in neutral. The left pedal, when depressed, engaged low gear in the two-speed transmission. The middle pedal was content to do just one thing — put Mike in reverse, and the pedal on the right was quite simply the foot brake. There was no foot throttle on the early T's but some owners added them as an accessory.

Starting Mike by cranking was more complicated, and much more dangerous, than a rolling start. Usually Dib would sit in the driver's seat and a trusting friend would position himself in front of the radiator where the crank was. The cranker was extremely careful to keep his thumb tucked under his fingers so it (or even an arm) wouldn't get broken if the engine backfired ("kicked"), and just as careful to pull the crank up rather than push it down, for the same reason. The spark lever, too, had to be retarded (that means in the "up" position) to lessen the kick-back. If the hand brake wasn't back, the driver had to depress the left pedal halfway with his left foot, yet keep his right foot on the brake so he wouldn't run over the cranker when it did catch. It was rather like patting your head and rubbing your stomach at the same time.

As soon as the engine caught, the driver pulled the spark lever down and then the hand throttle was gradually eased down as needed. At this point Mike would sit there with the motor chugging while the cranker-passenger climbed in. The left pedal was pressed all the way down to low, and then the hand brake was released more or less in that order. When Mike was going fast enough (the cranker by now safely seated next to the driver in the cab, hopefully), Dib would let the left pedal come all the way out into high gear. Mike would be at this point traveling at the approximate speed of ten or fifteen miles an hour.

Once the car was started, the streets and hills of San Francisco were great for racing, a favorite pastime for Dib and his buddies. Mike would whip down the steep part of Balboa Street in great style, often beating younger cars to the bottom. On a warm evening some friend might say, "Let's see who can get to 25th Avenue first." Traffic in the late twenties being happily rather sparse, they would race down Balboa, one car along-side the other, zipping through all the inter-sections, never worrying about what might get in the way. Once Dib came down 41st from Anza to Balboa boasting to a friend

with him that he could cross Balboa without touching the brake. He would have been able to do it, too, if a streetcar hadn't arrived at Balboa at the same time he did. Bets aside, Dib tried every trick he knew to get Mike to stop. He raised the gas lever, put on the foot brake, even stepped on the left pedal to shift into low gear. None of these things stopped Mike, though, and the only way Dib avoided a collision was to make a sharp right turn as hard and fast as he could. Mike skidded right up next to the streetcar and followed it along, broadside, for a hundred feet, before finally stopping. Some drivers of T's used reverse as a brake, but Dib was going too fast (and his feet and hands were too busy already) to use it that time.

Dib's good buddy Tod Snedeker sometimes went along on such rides, al-though often reluctantly. He was most happy working on cars, not racing them. One time Dib talked him into seeing how fast Mike could go along a flat stretch of road at the beach called the Great Highway. A friend in a car with a speedometer drove alongside and clocked Mike at over fifty miles an hour, not a bad showing, especially since the top speed for a Model T even in its prime was supposed to be about forty-five miles an hour.

Mike served the Fewer family admi-rably, despite the racing and the spark plug whistle, until that spring of 1931, when Dib and Tod agreed to give the old car its own special road test, across the U.S. of A. and back again.

CHAPTER TWO

Mike Gets Ready

Before starting out on a motor camping tour look over the tool box and see that it contains the necessary wrenches, such as open end wrenches, an adjustable (or monkey) wrench, a Stillson wrench and a spark plug socket wrench; a pair of pliers; also chain-repair pliers; a mechanics hammer; a large and small screwdriver; files; a spool of soft iron wire; a box each of assorted nuts, bolts and cotterpins; a box of extra tire valves; a tire pressure gauge; some extra spark plugs and rim lugs; a box of talcum powder; a few feet of high and low tension cable; a roll of tape; an extra valve and spring; a grease gun; an extra spring clip and bolts; an extra fan belt; a sheet of cork for emergency gaskets and a small bottle of shellac.

— 1926 *Rand McNally Auto Road Atlas of the United States*

Dib and Tod might have convinced themselves that the trip was a good idea, but nobody on earth could convince Tod's mother that it wasn't the end of her youngest son, the last of her four children still at home. She thought he would never come back, that the Indians would get them, or they would break down in the middle of the desert and starve. And she wasn't too sure about the gangsters either. From what she had seen, they were all over the Midwest, shooting innocent people at random.

Tod tried to explain that it was just a vacation but she wouldn't hear it. After that first conversation they just didn't discuss it anymore.

Both young men were living at home. Tod made $50 a month at the California Ink Company and Dib earned about $40 a month as a salesman for a wholesale hardware firm. They opened a joint savings account and started putting as much money as they could into it each week. Tod's first contribution was the $35 he got for selling the Essex. (He sold it to an unsuspecting Italian immigrant at the ink company who didn't know how to drive yet.)

Each weekend in June and July they did something more to improve Mike for the trip. For the first major overhaul Tod put in a Delco ignition and spark coils, a much better ignition system than the one that came with the Model T's.

Like everything else on the car, the original ignition was extremely simple. It used the current from a magneto, actually a set of horseshoe-type magnets secured to a flywheel. The magnets revolved with the flywheel, generating current that was transmitted into the spark coils, where it was boosted and then sent to the spark plugs to ignite the fuel mixture. The four coils were housed in a box below the dashboard on the inside of the cab. All the time the engine was going, there was a constant flow of current — the faster the magneto ran, the more energy was generated. When operating you could hear the coils going Zit-Zit-Zit-Zit, and the box was hot from the electric charge. If anyone touched the coil wires, he would get a shock, not painful, but a shock nonetheless. These temperamental coils had to be adjusted just so, and frequently, and one of their drawbacks was that they were always slipping out of adjustment.

The new Delco system sent all of the juice through a distributor, which in turn serviced all the spark plugs from one point, smoothing out the entire system immensely and eliminating entirely the coils and the box. Tod gave Mike an automatic starter at the same time, which meant they had to invest in a battery to charge it. This didn't mean they didn't use the crank anymore. It just meant they didn't have to use it as often.

To increase gas mileage Tod installed a quarter-inch petcock on the intake manifold. With the petcock, on the open road, the passenger could lean out his side of the car and open it up so that Mike was burning a leaner fuel mixture (gas mixed with air). It saved a great deal of money although it probably wasn't particularly good for Mike's gas line and carburetor. This only worked on flat ground or slight grades, too, and it wouldn't work around town at slow speeds. Tod was convinced it would save them gas

The Ferry Building in San Francisco at the end of Market Street circa 1931, when Dib and Tod started their trip.
There is a decided lack of a Bay Bridge, not to be completed until 1936.
Courtesy of the San Francisco Public Library.

in the long run, though.

They resecured Mike's front fenders with a cable that wrapped around the radiator cap. It wouldn't do to have Mike coming apart on the way to New York City and the lights of Broadway. Since the original windows had been broken, they developed some makeshift side curtains out of celluloid. They could either be put all the way up and strapped in place or stored behind the seat. There was no in between. But they would serve well enough in bad weather.

Dib's father gave them two almost new Sears tires for the rear wheels. The Model T's original "clincher" tires were very narrow — 30" x 2" in the front and 30" x 3-1/2" in the back (for better traction). Wider tires, which were about 30" x 5-1/2", were introduced in the last few years of Model T manufacture. They were a couple inches rounder than the earlier tires.

Clincher tires were all pretty narrow, much like bicycle tires, with wooden spoked wheels for a frame and inner tubes to hold the air. They fit onto a fixed clincher rim that grabbed the inflated tire and held it in place. The airstem from the innertube poked through to the outer rim of the wheel. Dib located two pretty good tires for the front, and four passable ones for spares to be tied onto the turtleback, all of the later model and the same width so Mike was evenly shod.

Then came the task of converting the Lizzie into a traveler. They built cabinets on the passenger side of the cab to the rear of the door to house their plates, cups, and cooking things. The porcelain plates were strapped to the back of the cabinet with rubber bands, and the cups sat on the shelves, secured by pieces of wood so they wouldn't rattle. Tod drilled a hole in the handle of the frying pan and bolted it in place with a wing nut.

The whole cabinet rested on the running board on the passenger side, against the rear fender. The door of the cabinet opened down and was held by a chain so that it lay flat to make a table. Everything they needed to cook with, except the two-burner Coleman stove, was kept in the cabinet. Tod got cans of every size and shape from the factory where he worked to store food and water — friction-top cans and cans with lids that fit snugly to keep out rain, dust, and bugs. Everything had its place — all the essentials, sugar, flour, salt, and pepper were in labeled cans.

In addition Dib constructed a wooden box big enough to hold three square gallon cans — one for gas, one for water, and one for oil. It just fit on Mike's running board on the driver's side. They also strapped an extra five-gallon can of water on top of the cabinet for emergency use in the desert.

Two canvas folding cots were fastened onto the turtleback of the cab (for sleeping away from damp ground and rattlesnakes or lizards), as well as an old washpan and two campstools that would be handy. But what proved to be the most handy was a 12" x 20" unpainted wood box they called the "junk box" that was filled with all the automobile miscellanea Tod and Dib had collected to fix cars — a lot of things Rand McNally's atlas recommended, and some things McNally never thought of, including a dime to measure the spark plug gaps and distributor points . . . just in case it did take more than a screwdriver, pliers, and some baling wire to keep Mike going.

Outside on the driver's side where the extra gas, water, and oil cans were stored in a box, they bolted a stretch-out luggage carrier. It opened like an accordion and went the length of the running board, and inside it they corralled their sleeping bags and two suitcases, both covered with fitted homemade oilcloth covers. This meant that the driver's door couldn't be opened, but this didn't seem very unusual. The first Model T's had doors only on the passenger side, and many 1931 touring cars that carried four people had false doors on the driver's side that never had been nor were intended to be opened. Dib's dad helped them fashion sidepockets on the inside of each door for inside storage.

Special blanket flaps about fourteen inches long were sewn into the tops of their

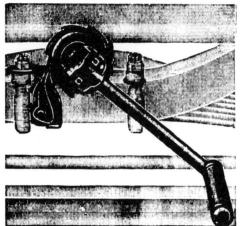
This 1922 "Non-Kick Device" automatically disengaged the clutch.
From Floyd Clymer's Historical Motor Scrapbook *Ford Model T Edition, Vol. 1. Courtesy Polyprint Publishing.*

cotton-filled sleeping bags for added warmth. They made another sheet that just fit inside that could be easily laundered, at least more easily than the bags. Two .22 caliber rifles and two fly rods were stowed in the cab, behind the seat, for hunting and fishing along the way.

Dib wanted to paint the name of each state they went through on Mike's cab as a record of the trip and Tod supplied some yellow paint for the job. Mike was already pretty well labeled. Across the back window were the words "Age Before Beauty," and "Mike" was painted in big letters on the front of the radiator (which had been painted silver). A decal on the right side of the windshield read "Let's Get Associated" — an advertising slogan of the Associated Oil Company. And in honor of the trip they painted the words "New York or Bust" below the windshield, for all the world to see.

Family and friends were very skeptical about their chances. Bets were made on how far the old heap would actually go before it ran out of steam — most bets gave them as far as Reno. The farthest bet allowed Denver, and that was a vote of confidence by Pinky, who had given Dib the Model T in the first place. He too was convinced Mike would be scrap metal after that.

In the middle of July they set the date of departure as August 3. By then they would have accumulated almost $150 in their joint bank account, and Mike was as ready as he ever would be for the trip. Then it was just a matter of deciding which direction to take.

In 1931 the two young men could have chosen seven different cross-country routes, not that any of them were very well maintained or even marked. It was quite a choice, compared to a few years earlier. It had been only twenty-eight years before, in

1903, when the very first successful auto trip from coast to coast was made by a brave pioneer in an early Winton. That driver had mostly wagon train routes to choose from. He started from San Francisco and traveled roughly, very roughly, 6,000 miles to get to New York City and back. It took sixty-three days, forty-five days traveling time, and he had to go from Sacramento through Oregon, over to Idaho, Wyoming, down through Omaha, Nebraska, to Chicago, Illinois, and then east to New York City, blazing his own roads a good deal of the way. From Kansas City east the roads were at least defined, if in terrible condition. But in the north and west he was on his own. Muddy cattle trails, treacherous wagon roads along steep mountains, and long, unmarked prairie had to be crossed, somehow.

It wasn't quite so rugged in 1931, but the roads were hardly smooth-riding across country, as Dib and Tod were to find out. At least they had a map they could use — the very first motorist used a "Blue Book" guide that literally described routes by using trees, barns, and rock formations as guidelines. It took almost a decade after the first coast-to-coast trip was made before anyone tried to connect the local roads into some kind of orderly route across the states. That was in 1912, when a group of wealthy men formed the Lincoln Highway Association to encourage a transcontinental highway from east to west. They provided the coordination and even money, and the local communities constructed the roads. The route was designated by using colored markers — an appropriate red, white, and blue for the "Lincoln Highway."

When the first edition of *Rand McNally's Auto Road Atlas of the United States* appeared in 1926, there were seven different routes across country, each marked by convenient colored markers. McNally charted them as: the Lincoln Highway, from San Francisco across the central part of the country to New York City; the National Old Trails Road, from Los Angeles to Washington, D.C. via part of the original Santa Fe Trail; the Theodore Roosevelt International Highway,

a northern route from Portland, Oregon, all the way to Portland, Maine; the Yellowstone Trail, marked with stones painted yellow, from Puget Sound on the West Coast north and east on the Canadian border to Plymouth Rock; Bankhead Highway, south and east through the southern states to Washington, D.C.; the old Spanish Trail, from California to Florida; and the Pikes Peak "Ocean to Ocean" Highway, from San Francisco to Philadelphia to New York.

Camping in the West had become very popular in the 1920s, mostly Model T camping, with elaborate tents strapped alongside Tin Lizzies' cabs. This had a good effect on some of the roads, and it certainly encouraged auto camps. A record 1,500,000 campers reportedly visited national parks in 1924. Auto camps sprang up everywhere to accommodate the crowds, Denver alone registering 800 camps in 1925.

The increased traffic didn't necessarily mean the roads were easier to travel, though. An account of a transcontinental trip in 1922 called *Modern Gypsies* by Mary Crehore Bedell said that "such fine sounding names as the Lincoln Highway, the Yellowstone Trail or the National Parks Highway may be misleading. Not yet can one spin across the continent on fine macadam, nor anywhere near it . . . the fact remains that most of the cross-country going is rather poor."

It wasn't until 1925 that the government decided to do something about overseeing roads across the country. That was the year the American Joint Board of Interstate Highways was appointed by the federal government. At their first meeting they abolished the old color-marked trails and roads and established routes across the country in a more orderly fashion. Routes from west to east were given even numbers; routes from north to south were given odd numbers.

Dib and Tod decided to start out on what had been called the Victory Highway but had been officially changed in 1925 to Route 40. It left San Francisco and headed more or less directly east, through the north-

ON Receiving Your Car, and before starting the motor, **Fill the Radiator** with clean, fresh water, preferably straining it through muslin or other similar material to prevent foreign matter getting into the small tubes.

It is important that the car should not even be run out of the freight car under its own power unless the circulating system is full. Pour in the water until you are sure both radiator and jackets have been filled and the water runs out of the overflow pipe. During the first few hours that the engine is running, it is a good plan to examine the radiator frequently and see that it is full and the water circulating properly. Soft rain water, when it is to be had in a clean state, is superior to water which may contain alkalies and other salts which are injurious, or which tend to deposit sediment and clog up the radiator.

Vigilance and Oil

THE first rule in motoring is to see that every part has, at all times, plenty of oil. The second is to see that every adjustment is made immediately the necessity of such adjustment is discovered.

The liability of trouble, with the consequent marring of pleasure trips through neglect to make adjustments promptly, increases by the square of the times they are neglected.

Permitting any part to run for even a brief period without proper lubrication will certainly result in serious injury to the machine and expense to the owner; and the results of reckless driving, while they may not show up immediately, will none the less certainly appear later for all that.

5

If the history of all the joyously anticipated pleasure trips that have ended disastrously could be written, it would be shown that in 90 per cent of the cases the humiliation and disappointment might have been avoided by making a certain repair and adjustment, the necessity of which was known before starting, instead of trusting to luck and a crippled part.

Go It Easy

IN the flush of enthusiasm, just after receiving your car, remember a new machine should have better care until she "finds herself" than she will need later, when the parts have become better adjusted to each other, limbered up and more thoroughly lubricated by long running.

You have more speed at your command than you can safely use on the average roads, or even on the best roads save under exceptional conditions, and a great deal more than you ought to attempt to use until you have become thoroughly familiar with your machine, and the manipulation of brakes and levers has become practically automatic.

Extraordinary conditions must be met when they present themselves—they should not be made a part of the every-day routine.

Gasoline

ALWAYS strain through chamois skin to prevent water and other foreign matters getting into the carburetor. When filling the gasoline tank, extinguish all lamps; throw away your cigar, and be sure that there are no naked flames within several feet, as the vapor is extremely volatile and travels rapidly. Always be careful about lighting matches near where gaso-

6

line has been spilled, as the air within a radius of several feet is permeated with highly explosive vapor.

Unless it has been tampered with, the carburetor adjustment is right, having been set by the head tester, so do not meddle with it until you are certain it needs adjusting. To make adjustment, manipulate button on dash—when leaving factory, adjustment is **O. K.,** and arrow points up. To give more gas, turn to left; for less gas, turn to right.

Lubrication

BEFORE your car is shipped the oil is drained out of the crank case. When ready to start, about a gallon of oil should be poured into the crank case through the breather pipe at the front of the engine.

There are two drain cocks in the flywheel casing or oil reservoir. The oil level should be carried between these two cocks. If it runs out of the upper, there is too much oil, and it should be allowed to drain out to that level. The oil level should never be allowed to fall below the lower cock. The oil in the crank case automatically oils cylinders, pistons, cam shaft, crank shaft bearings, connecting rod bearings, time gears and transmission.

The diagram shows the principal points of lubrication, and specifies when replenishment should be made, according to mileage. It is a good plan to frequently supply all oil cups with the same oil used in the engine (any lubricating oil will answer) and the dope cups with grease. When filling the dope cups, it is advisable to fill the cover, screw it down several turns and repeat the operation two or three times.

7

Always open oil cups by turning to right, as this keeps tightening rather than loosening them.

Occasionally remove front wheels and supply dope to wearing surface. A drop of oil now and then in crank handle bearing is necessary, also on fan belt pulleys and shaft. The axles, drive shaft and universal joint are well supplied with lubricant when the car leaves the factory, but it is well to examine them frequently.

The Kind of Oil to Use

WE recommend only light high grade gas engine oil for use in the Model T motor. A light grade of oil is preferred, as it will naturally reach the bearing surfaces with greater ease, and, consequently, less heat will develop on account of friction. The oil should, however, have sufficient body so that the pressure between the two bearing surfaces will not force the oil out and allow the metal to come in actual contact. Heavy and inferior oils have a tendency to carbonize quickly, also gum up the piston rings and valve stems.

Graphite or any form of heavy grease should not be used as a lubricant in the engine or transmission, as it will have a tendency to short-circuit the magneto.

Dope or grease should be supplied to the differential, front hubs and such other parts as indicated in diagram.

Control

ALL speeds are controlled by a foot pedal enabling the driver to stop, start, change speeds, or reverse the car, without removing the hands from the steering wheel. The foot pedal at the right, marked "B," operates the brake on the transmis-

9

sion. The pedal in the center, "R," operates the (reserve.) The left foot pedal, "C," is the control lever acting on the clutch.

The hand lever when thrown forward engages high speed; when pulled back, operates the emergency brake. The lever is in neutral when almost vertical and clutch is in a released condition. With the hand lever thrown forward in high speed, a light pressure on pedal "C," releases the clutch, while a full pressure on the pedal throws in the slow speed; by gradually releasing the pedal, it will come back through neutral into high speed.

Before Starting the Car, see that there is plenty of gasoline in the tank; the shut-off valve in the gasoline feed pipe open; the radiator filled; the proper amount of oil in

Showing the Simplicity of the Ford Left Hand Control.

10

the crank case; the grease cups, oil cups and other parts requiring lubrication given attention.

See that the hand lever is in a vertical position, the clutch thereby being disengaged and the emergency brake set.

Close the coil switch.

Place the spark lever at about the third or fourth notch of the quadrant—wherever the best results are obtained.

Open the throttle about five or six notches, and prime the carburetor if the engine requires it.

Engage the starting crank firmly and pull up on it. Two or three times will usually suffice to draw the mixture into cylinders and ignite it.

To Start the Machine, slightly accelerate the engine by opening the throttle, place the foot on the clutch pedal, and thereby hold the gears in a neutral position while throwing the hand lever forward; then to start the car in motion, press the pedal forward into slow speed and when under sufficient headway (20 to 30 feet), allow the pedal to drop back slowly into high speed, at the same time partially closing the throttle, which will allow the engine to pick up its load easily. With a little practice the change of speeds will be easily accomplished, and without any appreciable effect on the smooth running of the machine.

To Reverse the Car, it must be brought to a dead stop. With the engine running, disengage the clutch with the hand lever and press the reverse pedal forward with the left foot, the right foot being free to use on the brake pedal if needed.

To Stop the Car, partially close the throttle; release the high speed by pressing the clutch pedal forward into neutral;

11

apply the foot brake slowly but firmly until the car comes to a dead stop. Do not remove foot from clutch pedal, without first pulling hand lever back to neutral position. To stop the motor, open the throttle a trifle to accelerate the motor and then throw off the switch. The engine will then stop with the cylinders full of explosive gas, which will naturally facilitate starting.

Endeavor to so familiarize yourself with the operation of the car that to disengage a clutch and apply the brake becomes practically automatic—the natural thing to do in case of emergency.

When Driving the Car, the spark should be advanced as the speed increases until the engine reaches the highest point of efficiency. If the spark is advanced too far a dull knock will be heard in the motor, due to the fact that the explosion occurs before the piston has completed its compression stroke. The spark should only be retarded when the engine slows down on a heavy road or steep grade, but care must be exercised not to retard the spark to such an extent that over-heating will result. The greatest economy in gasoline consumption is obtained by driving with the spark advanced sufficiently to obtain the maximum speed. The varying speeds required to meet road conditions should be obtained by using the throttle, and with the wide range of flexibility which the Model T possesses there is very little occasion for releasing the high speed clutch or resorting to low gear under ordinary conditions.

The Cooling System

THE Cooling System of the Model T motor is known as the Thermo-Syphon or Gravity System, and acts on the prin-

12

ciple that hot water seeks a higher level than cold water, consequently when the water reaches a certain heat, approximately 180 degrees, circulation commences and the water flows from the lower radiator outlet pipe up through the water jackets into the upper radiator water tank, and down through the tubes to the lower tank to repeat the process. During the time that it is passing from the upper to the lower radiator tank it becomes cooled by the air which comes in contact with the fins and tubes of the radiator and which is sucked in by the fan. The rapidity of circulation is governed by the heat of the motor, and not by the speed.

Owing to the fact that circulation does not commence until the water becomes heated, it is advisable to use an anti-freezing solution in the circulating system in the winter, otherwise at low temperatures the water will be liable to freeze before it commences to circulate. Wood alcohol can be used to good advantage for non-freezing solutions and the following table gives the freezing point of solutions containing different percentages of alcohol:

20 per cent solution freezes at 10 degrees above zero.

30 per cent solution freezes at 5 degrees below zero.

40 per cent solution freezes at 20 degrees below zero.

50 per cent solution freezes at 55 degrees below zero.

A solution composed of 70 per cent water, 10 per cent glycerine and 20 per cent alcohol can also be used to advantage. Its freezing point is about 8 degrees below zero.

13

The T Instruction Book was full of practical information, as the owner was expected to drive, maintain, and most likely do major overhauls himself.

ern center of the country, over the High Sierras to Salt Lake City, joining the renumbered Lincoln Highway for a while, and then crossing the Rockies into Denver. Not that the decision was made with any kind of forethought. Basically, it was just the easiest way to head east from San Francisco — especially if, like Dib and Tod, you were curious to see the Sierra Nevada mountain range near San Francisco.

For a guide they used a Rand McNally atlas with individual pages for each section of the country. McNally showed the roads both with their old, more elaborate names and their new route numbers. It also indicated whether the roads were improved or unimproved.

Preparations complete, the August 3 departure date was going to work. They took the money out of the joint account — Dib was to be the banker — and left a small amount with Dib's mother in case they needed to wire for it while on the road.

The night before they left, a Sunday, Dib's folks gave them a going-away party. All their friends, including most of the local football team, the Richmond Rattlers, came to give them a good send-off, despite the fact that hardly anyone thought they would make it past the Rockies. Tod's family didn't participate: his mother didn't think the boys would make it back at all.

Everyone contributed something for the trip, nonetheless — home preserves, canned foods, dried beans, homemade cakes and cookies (from their girlfriends). The cakes were so numerous they were stacked three feet high on Mike's wood floorboards the next day. Dib's father donated two sides of bacon, the best he could find, and his mother gave them a half pint of bootleg bourbon, for medicinal purposes on the trip, she said.

With the teasing and betting and carrying on in general, it was a fine party, a wonderful goodbye for all three of them . . . Dib, Tod, and their Tin Lizzie, Mike.

CHAPTER THREE

Eastward Ho !

We plodded on, and at last the lake burst upon us, a noble sheet of blue water . . . walled in by a rim of snow-clad peaks that towered aloft full 3,000 feet higher still. As it lay there with the shadows of the mountains brilliantly photographed upon its still surface, I thought it must surely be the fairest picture the whole earth affords . . . Down through . . . these great depths, the water was not merely transparent, but dazzling, brilliantly so: we could see trout by the thousands winging about in the emptiness under us.

– About Lake Tahoe in *Roughing It*, by Mark Twain

The adventurers left San Francisco that first morning at 7:30, taking a ferryboat from the end of Market Street, across the bridge-less San Francisco Bay, all the way to Vallejo. (Dib and Tod reasoned strangely that they would save Mike's tires by going the few extra miles on water to Vallejo instead of Oakland, discounting thereby the thousands of miles still in front of them.) Dib wrote a penny postcard to his mom mailed from Vallejo August 3, "We're on the boat at present but nearly to Vallejo. Made connections fine & dandy. The ride has been darby."

Mike carried them over the summer-dry foothills of the coastal mountains, through broad Sacramento Valley farmlands check-ered with tomato, sugarbeet, and alfalfa fields. They were as good as outside, surrounded by outdoor smells through Mike's glassless window . . . rich, heady odors everywhere, some good and some not-so-good fertilizer smells from the cultivated land.

Their Lizzie worked like a champion all through the valley, running smoothly. At intersections in the small towns Dib and Tod would wait for the stop signal to clang and become green, and listen to the Ford chug contently in neutral. On the open road they opened the petcock to save gas.

By noon, the ninety miles to Sacramento were covered and they stopped for lunch at the home of "Aunt Rose," a friend of the Fewers. After a short visit, they drove through the sleepy, tree-lined streets to the State Capitol Building. Dib wrote cryptically in his journal, "After lunch we went to the Capitol — Revoked." Tod waited in front with Mike while Dib ran in to see if Governor Rolph wanted them to take a letter to Governor Roosevelt in New York via their marvel-ous Model T, but it was a last-minute thought and the governor wasn't even at the capitol that day. Dib wrote his mom, "Gov. was hunting, Sect. was out to lunch. I went right into his big office in my geans & no hat. What a darb: the crowd in the halls sure stared. But no letter." Hats were important in 1931. Tod had brought a narrow-brim felt one, which he would wear quite often. Dib had a tweed cap that he wore on occasion.

In August 1931, most of Route 40 was a two-lane highway, with an occasional stretch of three lanes, paved or "improved" all the way to Reno. It swung around the north side of Lake Tahoe and was labeled Lincoln Highway by Rand McNally. Another road out of Sacramento, also labeled Lincoln Highway by their atlas, skirted the south side and actually went closer to the lake, but it was "unimproved" from Tahoe to Reno and not the best choice for them.

In 1929 the official AAA Road Map showed five different categories of road: pavement (asphalt, brick, concrete, and hard-topped macadam, named after John Loudon Macadam, a nineteenth century Scotsman considered to be the founder of modern roads); improved (gravel, stone, shell, or sand clay); graded earth; earth (they cautioned the driver that this might sometimes be "bad during or following wet weather. Make local inquiry."); and proposed.

Heading east from Sacramento on the northern branch of the Lincoln Highway, the trio traveled steadily by the orchard-covered foothills of the Sierras, through Loomis, Newcastle, Auburn, and then climbed high into pine forest country. Mike did beautifully on the steep, winding grades, humming along at a reasonable fifteen or twenty miles an hour, only using low gear on the steepest parts. Dib confessed the Lizzie "boiled a little bit," but that was all. They cleared Donner Summit, and then went down to Donner Lake, where they settled for the night.

Despite the mountainous climb and the stop for lunch, they had traveled 180 miles this first day, climbing as high as 7,000 feet, with Mike using just nine gallons of gas and a half a quart of oil. Not a bad beginning to a long journey. And square and ugly as it was, the old Lizzie looked like it could carry them just about anywhere they wanted to go, including Broadway.

They were at a campground alongside the lake, right off Route 40, and had saved the fifty-cent fee. Dib explained in his letter of August 4, 1931, "Here we are at Donner Lake Auto Camp, free of charge as we had a letter from Armand at work to this kid up here. Nice fellow . . . Mike sure is a honey. It just roared over these high & mighty mountains with its heavy load."

Nonetheless, at the end of the first day, situated on the ground in the intense blackness and cold of a mountain lake, all was not tranquil for Tod. He had trouble sleeping, something that rarely happened to him. He no doubt was feeling the pinch of leaving home despite his mother's protests. She refused to admit that he was going . . . or even to say goodbye. And the whole idea did seem foolhardy. He and Dib had little money, really, according to their middle-class standards. If anything really went wrong, what

Mike all packed up for its first day on the road, parked in front of the state capitol in Sacramento and as yet still shiny.

would they do? They had talked about maybe earning more money as they went, working on farms if they had to, but neither of them had ever farmed. They were city-bred boys, much more adept at playing football than at pitching hay. The closest Tod had ever come to rural life was when he spent two summers on a ranch outside Santa Cruz when he was eleven and twelve. And although Mike performed like a trouper that first day, the Lizzie wasn't in perfect shape, by any means, as Tod knew better than Dib. It was an old, much used and abused car, and so many things could go snafu at any time. For example, just take that universal joint. What if it went . . . that was the end of the old Lizzie. And it could happen anywhere, out in the boonies, a thousand miles from a living soul. Or on top of a mountain somewhere. Or maybe in a desert, without water. Maybe his mom was right . . . maybe they had no business on this trip after all.

The next day, as it turned out, after a hearty breakfast of Dad Fewer's slab bacon, scrambled eggs, and homemade cake, every thing looked a lot rosier to Tod. After an extremely cold — hence very brief — swim in the shimmering blue water, they packed Mike in preparation for a side trip to Lake Tahoe. It was about twenty miles off the highway, and they would have to back-track to get on course again, but they'd been hearing about how darby Lake Tahoe was all their lives and they weren't going to miss it.

They found a spot for the night at Meeks Bay, an auto camp that looked almost deserted, and certainly unattended. Dib wrote in his journal, "Arrived at 2:45 in Meek's Bay,

Dib kept his journal in a stenographer's notebook in a clear, penciled handwriting. These are typical pages.

where we swam, plenty cold. Made camp in an auto camp. We thought it was free but we were caught and had to pay 50¢." That was a high price on their budget, especially because there weren't any true "facilities" like they might have expected in an auto camp. There was a dance floor, but no place to shower.

In 1931, many families from San Francisco went to the Russian River to vacation, which was only about sixty miles from the city. Clear Lake was also popular, about 100 miles away. But Tahoe, because of the distance, was considered quite an elegant and high-class place to visit. The enormous resort called Tahoe Tavern had been built around the turn of the century facing the lake, and lots of activities such as tennis, dancing, horse-

shoes, and horseback riding centered there. Rooms were expensive though, way beyond their means. There were a few auto camps and summer camps scattered about, but they cost quite a bit, compared to the "River" or Clear Lake. Dib remembers, "At Russian River we would rent a tent cabin. The ladies slept in that, and the fellows slept out in an area enclosed with burlap. It cost $35 a week." With camping alone costing fifty cents (without showers and other amenities), Tahoe was definitely high-class recreation.

On August 5 Dib wrote, "We're both sitting in Mike on the shore of the Lake looking out over the water. You would never know it was a Lake; it looks like S.F. Bay. It's about 1:00 p.m. and sure is nice and warm. Not much of a crowd here. About 100 on the

In his August 4, 1931 letter home, Dib sketches Mike, the spotlight, and even the music down the road.

beach. There are 2 speedboats roaring out on the lake. We slept good last night and had peaches, eggs, bacon and coffee at 8:30 a.m. We've been swimming and beat a couple champs up here in horseshoes already.

"It sure is nice . . . if the gang were . . . here it would be as good as the River. We sat in the free dance last night to get our 50¢ worth for the camping. Will have to sleep someplace else tonight I guess."

Letters home became, at this point and for the rest of the trip, a somewhat edited version of the truth. The truth was they had both slept cold the night before, and with very little pushing from Tod, who hated the hard ground, they decided to sleep in Mike that night, both to save the camping fee and keep warm.

There were, in 1931, many national park tourist campsites across country. Rand McNally glowingly described them: "The sites are often situated in spots of great natural beauty at the foot of wooded hills or rugged mountains, on the edge of a majestic forest, on the shore of a rippling lake or on the bank of a stately river, sometimes overlooking a valley where lies the city with its distant hum by day and its twinkling lights by night . . . Information regarding the location of camp sites is easily secured. Signs erected in the towns and near them will point the way. . . Tourists' camp sites are free." Unfortunately for Dib and Tod, no sign had pointed the way

Mike with all the camping gear, rear view, probably taken in the parking lot at Donner Lake.

and there wasn't a tourist site in sight. They were forced to sleep in the Model T.

It turned out, however, that the least of Mike's virtues was being adaptable to a comfortable night's sleep. The coupe was a decent size for riding, the spring seats reasonably bouncy, but for two young men the size and shapes of Dib and Tod, there just was no position that was exactly stretched out. Six-foot-tall football players just didn't fit. They spent most of the night trying to adjust to the space.

August 6 they left Lake Tahoe about 9:30 in the morning, heading back through Tahoe City to pick up Route 40 east again. The highway twisted in and out between overhanging ledges, down through the Truckee River Canyon, and then across the border into the dry, rocky sagebrush desert of the state of Nevada. The top surface was good and Mike was in fine fettle. They sped along at good speed, undoubtedly hitting that magical fifty miles an hour, although they couldn't be sure without a speedometer.

Again the petcock was opened, and apparently this worked well, because they continued to do it and Dib wrote a day or so later, "We traveled 200 miles today . . . (and) used 9 gals . . . what mileage. Of course you'll say it's baloney."

They stopped briefly in the town of Reno, passing up the opportunity of gambling at the newly opened game tables, and wrote a card August 6: "This is Thurs. noon. Just arrived in Reno. We expect to go right through. Entered Nevada at 11:30 P.S.T. Mike is sure a darb. Gas costs 20 1/2 cents up here." Dib noted P.S.T. (Pacific Standard Time) anticipating the one-hour difference when they crossed into Mountain Time later in Utah.

They found a place to sleep the night about twenty miles on the other side of Reno close to Wadsworth, on the banks of the Truckee River. The "water was lousy and stagnant" unusable for either drinking or swimming, "the prairies . . . dry with scrubby bushes." But there was a tree and they "had an afternoon sleep in the shade" since it was early, quite hot, and dry, and there wasn't much else to do.

When they woke, Tod got the .22 rifles from the back of the cab, and they walked into the sagebrush to do some jackrabbit hunting. They had seen them everywhere on the desert, especially flattened on the highway. The two young men reasoned a gunshot was a much more dignified way to meet the Maker than the front end of a Ford or Packard.

The ubiquitous bunnies appeared darting from bush to bush. Tod hit one on his third shot with his .22 special that required longer bullets but was a little more accurate than Dib's. Tod was in charge of skinning the rabbit that night, and Dib took over frying the hind legs in bacon grease over the Coleman stove. It made a great camp meal, and it wasn't until after supper, when Tod wanted to finish off supper with a smoke, that he remembered he had set his favorite pipe down in the excitement, out somewhere in the desert.

Friends had warned them about poisonous snakes and lizards in this kind of country, so that night they set up the cots for the first time. It had been a hot day, and they figured that down from the mountains they would finally get a warm night's sleep. But it was freezing, once again, and the air under the cots made them even colder. They were getting used to discomfort by now, though, and slept well. They were up, decamped, and on the road by 7:30 — and that included Tod getting another rabbit. Both of them had lucky left hind feet for the trip now — certainly a good omen.

They hadn't gone far before the good, well-paved highway they had traveled since leaving San Francisco changed, drastically, and "Mike had to labor in low gear plenty on the 'under construction' roads." According to their Rand McNally, the roads outside Reno were supposed to be "improved." "Improved," they discovered that day, meant that the road had been scraped by a scraper so that the big potholes were filled in, sometimes covered with rough gravel, and possibly rolled over with a heavy roller. It meant, too, that the first few cars across the surface left tire marks deeply embedded, so that future cars were

almost required to follow the same ruts.

Dib remembers, "We'd see more graders and scrapers than cars . . . in most cases where (they) were working there was gravel or clay or whatever. And so with the erosion of weather and wind they had to go through frequently to grade and scrape it . . . make it level again, instead of potholes. . . . that's why we had so many detours. They were always working on the highway, because it wasn't paved."

They were still on Route 40, now suddenly changed from the Lincoln to the Victory Highway. That first day in Nevada they went through Miriam, Toulon, "Lovelocks" (misnamed, apparently, in the book and actually called Lovelock), Oreana, Rye Patch, Imlay, Mill City, Rose Creek, Golconda, Iron Point, Herrin, and Stonehouse to Battle Mountain, 200 bone-rattling miles. At one point they hit construction work that lasted twenty-five miles, Mike using low gear the whole way. And twenty-five miles could seem like a century at five and ten miles an hour.

Good travel time was not what they made that day . . . or the next. Mike bounced along at ten miles an hour at best, a fair speed given the washboard road conditions. To keep the engine cool, Tod opened the hood on both sides of the engine, tucked the lids under, and fastened them with a rope so the wind would go right through and around the motor. This made it easy to make adjustments on the motor while they were moving. Mike almost looked like it had wings. And to keep their gas mileage low, they opened the petcock whenever they could. The Ford had a layer of dust so thick it didn't look black anymore, and the roads made it shake like it had the "agge," Dib later wrote home.

Again they felt the immensity of the distance they were attempting to travel. Dib and Tod joked about how long it would take them to get to Broadway if all the roads east turned out to be like this interminable stretch of U.S. 40.

They slept in a baseball field one night, another night in a farmer's field, worried that the farmer would at any moment discover and shoot them for trespassing. Some bulls

Tod models his lisle racing suit at Meek's Bay, Lake Tahoe.
Much lighter than the more widely used wool swimsuits,
it dried almost immediately. Notice zinc ointment on
his nose to avoid the mile-high sun.

A typical Nevada road in 1931, dirt and gravel, but Mike looks
ready, bent fender and all. Not a tree in sight.

did chase them, but they scrambled into Mike and got away in time.

On August 8 Dib wrote home, "Three cheers, here we are in Elko, Nev. 3 o'clock Sat. aft. We left Battle Mt. 11 a.m. this morn as I said we slept in a baseball field, the night was cool and quiet. Nearly all the cars were old fords. The reason is gas is 25¢. The same in Elko. We had 5 gals when we left Battle Mt. and to Elko its around 76 miles. We haven't looked at the gas yet."

Dib and Tod quite literally "looked" at the gas. The only way to check it was to take off the seat cushion that was over the cylindrical tank and dip a stick in to see how much fuel was left. This meant unless you wanted to get out, remove the cushion, and dip in a stick all the time, you had to remember how far you had gone since you filled up last. There wasn't any warning should gas get real low. If you wanted a measure more accurate than just dampness, you could mark a stick with the number of gallons on it.

Dib continued, "We had more terrible blankety blank roads from Battle Mt. to Elko, also pretty stiff hills. Well, we're feeling fine and after oiling and gas we'll continue. No trouble so don't worry."

Except for crossing through some lower hills, the scenery changed little, mile after dusty mile, and as a rule the only things seen moving besides themselves in Mike were numerous prairie dogs, some soaring hawks, the ever-present rabbits, and an occasional auto, usually a Ford of one kind or another (probably because of the expensive gas; Lizzies didn't use much). Tiny desert towns were no more than way stations, dispensing gas out of round, green-glassed pumps, charging what Dib and Tod considered to be exorbitant prices. Sometimes it was as high as twenty-seven cents a gallon, double the city price, and if they wanted water or air they had to pay for it.

Dib wrote his mom from Wells on Sunday, August 9, "Yesterday, (Sat.) we traveled near 119 miles over bum, hilly roads. We used low gear plenty because Mike couldn't get a start and didn't have any traction. Not a flat so far or a speck of trouble. Believe it or not we used 4 1/4 gals for 119 miles. If the road was smooth and flat we wouldn't have to buy gas (which is still 25¢). We have the intake petcock wide open. Also travel with doors and windows open."

Every group of buildings, no matter how small, seemed to have a name . . . Vivian, Halleck, Deeth, Cobre, Silver Zone. If the days were exceptionally long, hot, and dusty, the evenings were pleasantly spent around the stove or a bonfire, learning how to make suppers their mothers would be proud of — stews and hash and beans and any number of things they had never had to cook before. Everything tasted delicious in the open air,

too. Dib and Tod learned to be conservative with their foods, alternating mornings so that one day they would have two eggs each with the bacon they had wrapped in a sack, next day they would use just one egg and make pancakes for breakfast. Tod even convinced Dib his oatmeal tasted as good with syrup on it as with sugar (and introduced him to canned milk on oatmeal).

They had planned well and were adequately supplied for the waterless desert miles. The five-gallon can served for washing between watering spots, and aside from the dismal roads, both of them were enjoying the journey. With each mile they were getting more road wise. A gas station attendant who had bummed his way across the country told them to use newspapers to help insulate their bags. That night they put papers between the bags and the cots and found it worked well.

Missing good exercise, every night before they went to sleep they devised an exercise regime on top of the sleeping bags to keep up their football muscles: seventy- five pushups and seventy-five situps. They hun-

Camping out, Mike serves them well. The table is down, pantry open for business, and all the containers, enamel cups and plates, still new and clean. As yet, there is no newspaper under their bags. The unlucky jackrabbit is tied to the right front fender. Dib is just waking in the early morning on the desert.

gered for a good swim, too, and when they crossed from Nevada into Utah at Wendover, Dib asked an attendant, "Hey, got any swimming tanks around here?" The attendant, standing in the middle of one of the driest spots in the dry West, just shook his head back and forth slowly and looked at Dib as if he were crazy.

HOW TO MEASURE FUEL IN A ROUND MODEL T GAS TANK

(*From* The Ford Times, 1912)

Here's a little diagram that will tell you easily and accurately exactly how much gasoline is in the tank of your touring car. How many times can you remember, when it would have come in handy to have known just how many gallons of gasoline you had? A little care in marking on a stick the figures on the accompanying table will provide a means of always knowing your exact supply.

You frequently have dipped a stick in your tank and told by the damp surface of the stick how deep the gasoline was. With a stick supplied with the figures from the chart shown, you can see at a glance how many gallons are left in your tank.

Those who take the trouble to prepare themselves this handy little measuring rod will not regret the labor. It may save them from a chagrining delay along the countryside for want of "gas."

[*Later such sticks were turned out by the millions and given away as advertising souvenirs.*]

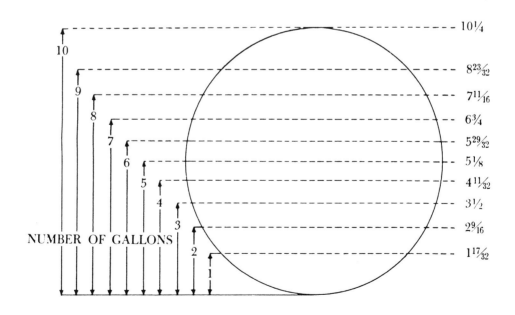

Diagram showing the correct measurements in gallons and inches of the ten gallon tank used on Ford touring cars.

The first Model T owners had to make their own dipsticks, but later Ford made them as an advertising gimmick and gave them away by the millions.
From the Ford Times, 1912.

CHAPTER FOUR

The Joys of the Road

Now the joys of the road are chiefly these;
A crimson touch on the hardwood trees;
A vagrant's morning wide and blue,
In early fall when the wind walks, too;
A shadowy highway cool and brown,
Alluring up and enticing down

— *Bliss Carman (From the cover of a pamphlet titled*
How's the Road *by Kathryn Hulme, 1928)*

"Here we are, right in the Pink in Salt Lake City," Dib wrote his mom August 11, 1931. "We stopped at Nelson's Camp here in the City. The main attraction was showers and shade. We're all nice and clean now. We sure had a darby trip." He loved the road, even if it was bumpy. Mike was running like a "champ," despite the "cheesy" highways that were loose gravel and washboard, making Mike jump and toss them around. This didn't bother them, though. They were seeing country they'd never seen before, and every day was an adventure.

They arrived in Salt Lake City on Monday, August 10, collecting their first mail from home at the General Delivery window at the main post office. This inspired them to sit down near Mike and write family and friends about their adventure so far. Dib described their first glimpse of Utah: "As we came over the hill at Wendover we gazed at a vast expanse of shiny white desert. The

deserts so far have been sage, but this was absolutely white salt. We couldn't see the other side . . . Well, we pushed off about 3 p.m. to cross the desert. The roads are still terrible. It took us nearly 4 hours to cross the 45 miles . . . (we had coffee and helped a fellow with his tire during this time.) After crossing (into Utah), the roads improved a little but then got as bad as ever. 'Mike' takes it all as a matter of fact. Not even a flat."

Taking four hours to cross just forty-five miles was a concern to them because it ruined their overall "average" mileage. And doing well with the mileage was one of the whole points of the trip.

In the same letter he wrote, "From Wells to Wendover we used 2 1/2 gals. About 65 miles over bum ???!!! Roads. From Wendover to here we used 4 1/4 gals. About 135 miles. Gas is 20 1/2¢ (3 cheers)."

Dib remembers, "Most of the towns were very narrow, a lot of dirt streets. It (Salt

Lake) had streams of water running down the streets. . . always had water running down the gutters to keep the temperature down and to keep it clean. Buildings were clean. We were impressed. . ."

Salt Lake City was their first city since San Francisco, and it sure felt good to see people again. Lots of them. Not to mention the pretty girls.

They were staying at an auto camp on the outskirts of the city called Nelson's. For fifty cents a night they had a shady place to park and the use of a wood stall shower and a laundry area where the management supplied a water pump and large tubs for them to wash out their dusty clothes.

Auto camps came in all sizes and types in 1931. Many were quite elegant; many far from it. Public shower areas were often wooden stalls with water heads that dribbled water onto the showerer. . . sometimes warm, sometimes not. Laundry areas were large enough to accommodate several people, with clotheslines for auto campers to hang wet things on. For a modest fee you bought the use of the facilities and the grounds. Some camps had cabins for rent as well – often very rustic – for about $1 a night. The more elegant camps even had cabins with kitchens. Occasionally you would find miniature golf courses or dance halls, and horseshoe pits were a common attraction.

Mike and those other 15,000,000 Model T's were a chief reason these useful places had sprung up across the country. In the twenties, when the Model T was getting around very well and all over, more and more people of modest means were traveling longer distances on vacation, exploring areas they wouldn't have been able to reach before. In the Lizzie it was economical, because like Mike, they didn't burn much gas, and if you bought a special tent that attached to the side of the car, it was reasonably comfortable. When locals found they could charge a few cents for letting these autos park and use their water, the idea of an auto camp just naturally evolved.

Salt Lake City was the first big city they came to and was quite impressive,
certainly a contrast to what they had seen thus far.
Courtesy of the Utah State Historical Society

Nelson's in Salt Lake City was quite comfortable, with plenty of shade trees. And if the shower dribbled instead of spraying, Dib and Tod didn't mind. The water felt too good. They had five days of dust to wash away, and they took as many showers as was decently possible. Mike wasn't that lucky. By now the old Ford looked like it had a white "tan" from all the dust it had accumulated. And they couldn't clean the car up because of all the camping gear fastened to the sides.

They rested at Nelson's for two days. To make sure Mike was ready for the next long pull east, a local mechanic took a look at the engine. Everything was hunky-dory, just as expected.

On August 12, just nine bumpy days since leaving San Francisco, well washed and well fed, they set out again on Route 40, heading toward Broadway. At a mountain town about forty miles southeast of the city, Dib wrote a postcard home: "Again we meet, we just pulled into Heber, Utah. Small town & saddle horses are on the main st. We turn here & it looks like gravel roads. All the way from Salt Lake, about 60 miles, we had good road. We also had our first flat. We had to throw the tire away as the ridge that fits in the rim tore loose. It was an old front one." At this point Mike's "shoes" began to go. All of the detours and pitted roads finally caught up with the old car.

Outside Heber they heard a bang,

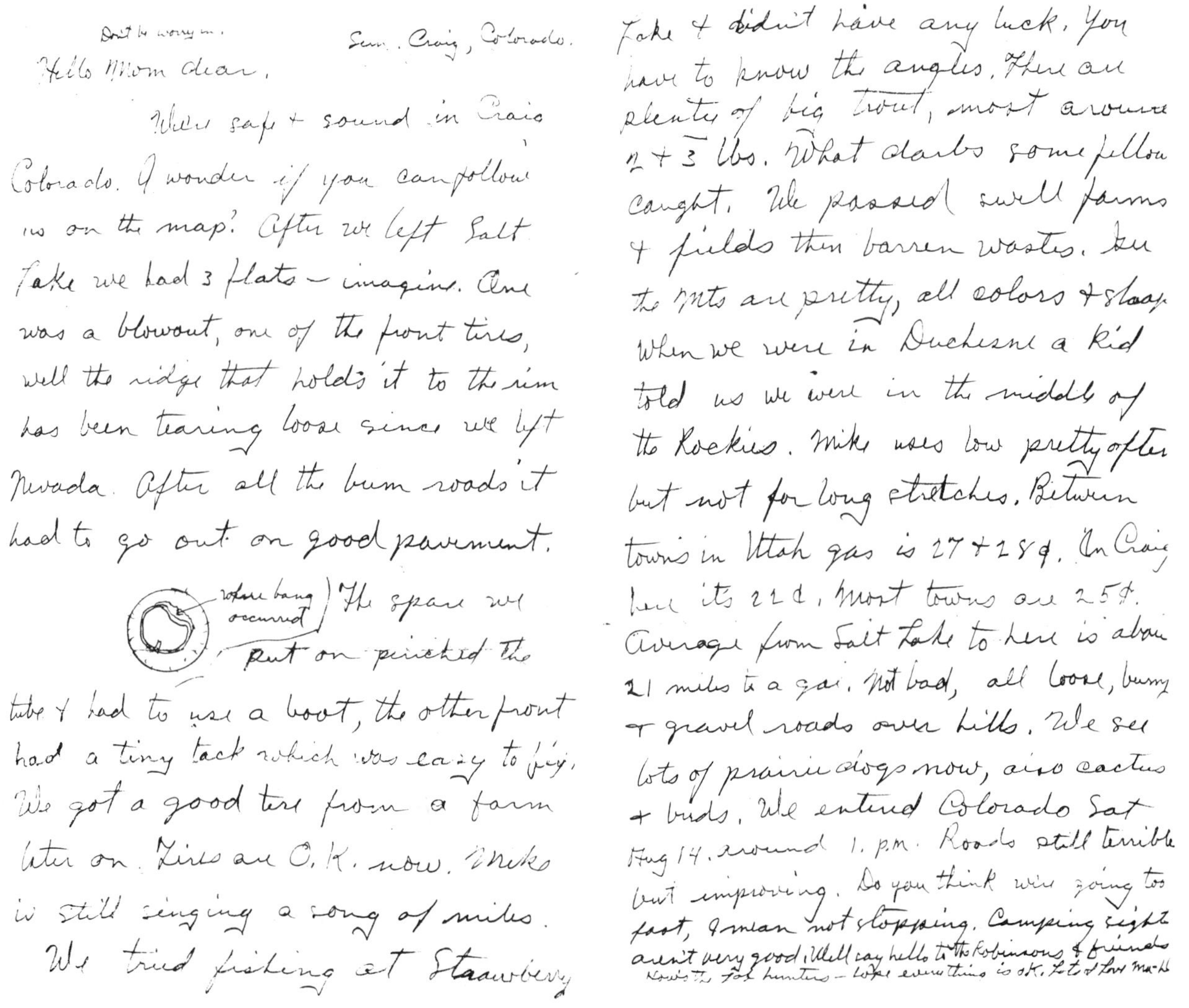

[Handwritten letter]

Don't be worry me .

Hello Mom dear,

Sun. Craig, Colorado.

We're safe & sound in Craig Colorado. I wonder if you can follow us on the map? After we left Salt Lake we had 3 flats — imagine. One was a blowout, one of the front tires, well the ridge that holds it to the rim has been tearing loose since we left Nevada. After all the bum roads it had to go out on good pavement. The spare we put on pinched the tube & had to use a boot, the other front had a tiny tack which was easy to fix. We got a good tire from a farm later on. Tires are O. K. now. Mike is still singing a song of miles. We tried fishing at Strawberry Lake & didn't have any luck. You have to know the angles. There are plenty of big trout, most around 2 + 3 lbs. What darbs some fellow caught. We passed swell farms & fields then barren wastes. Out the mts are pretty, all colors & shaped. When we were in Duchesne a kid told us we were in the middle of the Rockies. Mike uses low pretty often but not for long stretches. Between towns in Utah gas is 27 + 28¢. In Craig here its 22¢, most towns are 25¢. Average from Salt Lake to here is about 21 miles to a gal. Not bad, all loose, bumpy + gravel roads over hills. We see lots of prairie dogs now, also cactus + birds. We entered Colorado Sat Aug 14, around 1. pm. Roads still terrible but improving. Do you think we're going too fast, I mean not stopping. Camping sights aren't very good. Well say hello to the Robinsons & friends ...

[annotation on tire diagram] where bang occurred

Dib's August 17, 1931 letter home showed Mike's tire off the rim and told them, in detail, about the flats they had.

and Mike began to wobble. Ever since they had left Nevada the molding that held the tire to the rim had been tearing loose, so they were expecting it to go flat. They used one of the many spares strapped to Mike's back to replace it.

About five miles later Mike went thumpety-thump once again. . . the same front tire was gone again. This they didn't expect, because it was a good tire as far as they could tell. But when they looked at it they discovered the tube had been accidentally pinched when the spare was put on the rim, causing it to crack and lose air. Easy to fix. Dib patched the tube with a rubber patch they found in the junk box, and they were on the road again. . . at least for a while.

Ten more miles down the road Mike once again started to wobble, and the trio bounced over to the side of the road one more time. This time the other front tire had picked up a tack. Tod patched it, and they were on their way again in record time, climbing in low gear now, up into the majestic mountains before them. As the tire supply was getting low, they bought one from a farmer for a few cents and strapped it on Mike's back for future use.

Dib changes the tire, exposing big, homemade side pocket with the door open. The hood is folded under, the split windshield open, to let the old T have lots of air.

Flat tires were to be expected. That's why Mike hauled so many spares. It was also expected that you would have to patch them, or possibly stop and help a fellow traveler patch his.

A flat tire could be patched in any number of ways. If a hole wore through the outer tire, eventually the inner tube would pop out and be cut or get a hole and the tire would deflate. But just because a tire had a gaping hole in it didn't mean it was discarded. There were all sorts of ways to patch the inside of the tire and strengthen the hole so the tire could go a few more miles. A "boot" could be made out of a lot of things — canvas, leather, bits of other tire. But there were also ready-made boots that had tacks or glue on one side to fix them to the inside of the tire casing so they wouldn't slip around. The tacks pressed into the tire itself, and the tube rested against the smooth part of the boot on the inner side. Powder kits called "hot patches" actually burned the patch onto a tube with gunpowder, sulphur, or an inflammable material that was embedded right into the patch. A tube could also be fairly easily patched with stick-on patches called "cold patches" wherever the air escaped. A tire might have three, four, or more patches or boots, and the tire's tube might have four or five patches as well . . . and there might even be a few patches on top of patches.

Dib recalls, "A tire would wear off not overall but would be worse in one area. And when the tube was about to show, there was a tube inside, a very delicate thing, you would put in an innersole . . . an inner patch, and that would protect the tube from the opening in the tire. Just like a shoe, you would feel a bump when you walked along, and the same with the car." Tod adds, "In the good old days you wore your shoes until they got a hole in them . . . then you'd put a piece of cardboard or a piece of anything you could get inside . . . you tried to get the most out of what you had."

Such makeshift tires weren't dangerous, really, because the usual speed of a Model T was about thirty to thirty-five miles an hour on the road. And even when a tire had a sudden blowout while the car was going thirty-five miles an hour, nothing too much could go wrong because the Model T had a three-point suspension system that made it very flexible on uneven roads, and difficult to throw out of balance. (Except, of course, if it were hit by another car or knocked over onto its side somehow, as Mike had been. Then it was rather like a turtle turned over on its back, unable to right itself.)

Three flat tires didn't help their traveling time much that day. The plan was to stop a few days, anyway, about sixty miles outside Salt Lake at a lake reputedly great for fishing. Dib wrote home, "We heard of a good camping and fishing place in Strawberry Lake, so if we go there, maybe for a week, we might not write, so don't worry." By the time they reached the dirt entry road to the reservation, they had climbed 8,000 feet, higher than they had been so far. Mike used an uncommon five gallons of gasoline to do it.

The reservation was alive with sage hens and rabbits, and if fish were as plentiful, they would soon be tasting some darby mountain trout fried in butter. A sudden rain squall caught them, their first rain on the trip, and they put up the celluloid side curtains to keep the water out. Luckily the rain quit before they turned in.

That night, in the middle of a dream about playing football, Dib was awakened suddenly by a heavy weight on his foot. At first it was part of his dream – a particularly big fullback had tackled him by grabbing his toe. He panicked when he opened his eyes in the intense darkness and realized it wasn't a dream. Tod felt it too, because he was scrambling for the flashlight they kept between them. He lighted it just in time to see an enormous frog, about twelve inches long, flip flop from Dib's bag, across his bag, and into the darkness.

Frost was heavy on their bags the next morning, and the cold, along with the anticipation of catching some big ones, woke them earlier than usual. By 6 a.m. they had

finished breakfast and were down at the wooden dock, arranging to rent a rowboat from a concessioner for $1, all day.

Fishing was not good for them that day, however, despite the fact that the lake was full of big trout, two and three pounders, Dib wrote in his journal. "(We) trolled from 6:00 to 1:00 p.m. We caught next to nothing, although there were woppers in the lake. All we got was a good tan. At 2:00 p.m. we left . . ." What made it more frustrating was that other fishermen were pulling in huge fish, and they couldn't catch a thing.

Dib remembers, "We stayed out a good percentage of the day trolling and doing this and that. We didn't see anybody catching any fish, either. And then we came in and these guys were holding up nice strings of lake trout or whatever they were, bass. We tried a lot of things for bait . . . spoons and lures, but we weren't fishing at the proper depth, and the guys that knew the lake came in with a whole pack of them."

Hard ground, frosty nights, and no luck weren't good combinations or any incentive to stick around, even if the fish were "woppers." They left that afternoon at 2:00 and got back on Route 40, driving through spectacular mountain country, east. Since it was late, they stopped after about fifty miles in a small town called Duchesne, and chose a campsite right on the Strawberry River, almost in the town itself. Strolling after dinner that night, Dib commented to a local boy, "Real pretty country round here." "No place like the Rockies," he replied proudly. Dib didn't let him know that it was news to them they were in the Rockies. . . their Rand NcNally atlas didn't tell them that bit of information. Besides, they were still in Utah, and had no idea the Rockies had already overtaken them. (Dib was still confused about the Rockies later in the trip and placed them in the Southwest, near Arizona, even farther from their true location.)

Next day, August 14, they drove through the small towns of Roosevelt and Vernal, and made camp that night along the banks of the Green River in Jensen, Utah. The biggest attraction there were about half a dozen pretty girls swimming in the river with an unexpected and appreciative audience of two young California travelers.

If they were impressed with the country and dames, the roads weren't impressing them favorably at all. Outside Jensen they hit a fifteen-mile detour that was only a sample of things to come. After the detour, the roads really got rough. Route 40's grades were steep, even a little scary at precipitous points where it dropped off into a deep gorge. Some of the most dangerous parts had been lined with a waist-high fence with poles placed about ten feet apart, two rather flimsy looking chains strung between to keep cars from going over. But most of the roads were dirt and unprotected. Dib and Tod had to use poor Mike's lowest gear, and the T labored up the mountain as slowly as it ever had moved – slow enough for Dib and Tod to take turns walking alongside to get some exercise while the other drove.

They were passing through beautiful country now. After the desert everything looked lush and green, especially to two native Californians who were accustomed to the dry hills around their native city in the summer and fall. Jagged mountain peaks were still capped with last winter's snow – just to keep the nights good and chilly for them.

In Craig, Colorado, August 17, 1931, Dib wrote his mother about the trip from Strawberry on: "We passed swell farms and fields, then barren wastes. Gee the mountains are pretty, all colors and shapes. When we were in Duchesne a kid told us we were in the middle of the Rockies. Mike uses low pretty often but not for long stretches. Between towns in Utah gas is 27 & 28¢. In Craig it's 22¢. Most towns are 25¢. Average from Salt Lake to here is about 21 miles to a gal. Not bad, all loose, bumpy & gravel roads over hills. We see lots of prairie dogs now, also cactus & birds." He enclosed a piece of cactus in the letter. "We entered Colorado Sat Aug 14 about 1 p.m. Roads still terrible but improving. Do you think we're going too fast, I mean not stopping. Camping sights aren't very good. Well say hello to the Robinsons & friends. How's the job hunters – hope everything is O.K. Lots of Love Ma — Dib."

"Too fast" apparently referred to not pausing to savor every town or vista, because they certainly weren't speeding.

A Colorado canyon in the Rockies, with a good look at a rope and post fence.

CHAPTER FIVE

Mike Tackles the Rockies

All in all we're having a wonderful time. Roads or no roads they're darby.

— Note to Dib's sister Gert August 19, 1931

Bacon sure is darby & we sure need the razors.

— Note to Mom & Pop, same day

After Steamboat Springs they started the steep ascent to the top of the continent — to Rabbit Ears Pass. Highway 40 crosses the Continental Divide at two points before reaching Denver, at Rabbit Ears and Berthoud passes. In 1931 it twisted like a snake, in and out, in and out, eventually winding its jagged way to the first 9,500-foot summit at Rabbit Ears. Mike worked hard for them but was doing okay, considering the condition of the road and the climb. Dib wrote home later from Denver on August 18 "I think I left you at Craig, Colo. Well we left there around Sun. noon. The roads are still terrible, detours, construction & just plain ??@! road. We soon hit the steep mountains. We got gas @ Steamboat Springs (20¢ a gal) & started up Rabbit Ear Pass — 9,500 el. Dirt road & winding in, out, in, out, all the way. We soon got a bird's eye view. Poor Mike used low all the way, about 1 1/2 hrs steady climb." At this point the old Ford used low

gear so long that all the water boiled away, an unusual occurrence.

The Model T's circulating system was called Thermosiphon and was designed to use natural force, which meant that when water was hot, it rose; when cooled, it sank. As water was heated by Mike's engine, it rose to the top of the radiator, replaced by cooler water from the bottom. Working as hard as it was in the Rockies, the Lizzie got hotter and so did the water.

It was on this laborious pull that Tod devised a way for both of them to exercise while Mike labored up the mountain without a driver in the cab. In order to keep the Ford in low gear, somebody's foot had to be holding down the left pedal, all the time, even if the car was going only a couple miles an hour. This was boring, if not taxing, so Tod located a stick alongside the road and put one end on top of the pedal and wedged the other end under the seat. After that the old Lizzie just kept chugging up the mountain all by itself, while Dib and Tod walked alongside. At curves, they reached through the window and turned the steering wheel . . . Mike was going so slowly it was easy to do, even with a lot of bends in the road.

In this snail-like and steady manner, they worked their way up to the divide. Only one or two other brave cars passed them that day, although around one curve they found two women struggling to fix a tire and stopped to help. Occasionally a road worker halted traffic in one direction for half an hour, and then another car or two would show up behind them. Otherwise they were alone, the three of them climbing the mountain.

When they came around a turn near the top, they discovered a work party, and tractors everywhere. A man directed them off the road, onto a detour that turned out to be nothing more than wild mountain. It was so rough that Tod and Dib, once again seated in Mike's cab, hit their heads a couple times on the top of the roof. (They learned to keep their heads down, shoulders crouched so they wouldn't get whacked.)

Dib and Mike climbing the Rockies on a fairly reasonable stretch of road.

All the miles were picturesque, if slow, but the last five miles of detours and construction before the summit were really rugged. Dib wrote, "At the top was dark clouds, also thunder & lightning. It sure is pretty country, trees & animals a change from deserts & farming. At the top was detours & construction for about five miles. Steam shovels, tractors, mules & scrapers all over. . . . Poor Mike. He's sure doing the work of a pack of mules."

Dib recalls, "Graders were similar to the ones they have now. A guy in a cab and he has a big blade out in front, and big tires, and he used that blade to scrape the road level, and dump gravel in potholes and crevices, and then he comes back and scrapes it again to make it hard."

Mike handled it like a mule, or a pack of them, as Dib wrote. Actually, the Model T had been engineered to travel just the sort of roads they were running into. When it was designed, in the first decade of the century, all the roads were chancy, if even existent, and outlying roads were never very smooth. A car had to be ready to take rough treatment. So Ford had designed a suspension system for the body that was much like the ones used on horse-drawn wagons.

The axle springs went from wheel to wheel, across the front and back wheels. That meant the Lizzie was loose jointed, and all four wheels could be bent at different angles and still keep rolling. Later, cars had suspension systems designed so that the whole car responded to the road in the same way, because the roads were more predictable. Mike could literally "walk" over bad roads. Of course, it wasn't too comfortable for the passengers inside, even considering the upholstered spring seat that could, on occasion, be bouncier than desired.

It clouded up that afternoon, getting ready for a nasty storm. By the time they reached the summit of Rabbit Ears Pass, it was getting dark and enormous drops of water were beginning to fall from the thick clouds. They intended to get away from the summit before making camp, but just as they began the descent, Dib stepped on the brakes and heard something click. When he tried the foot brake again nothing happened. He tried the hand brake, but Mike just kept rolling. Then he tried hitting all three pedals at once. Still nothing. The car was just moving along again, all by itself, with nothing to stop it.

Tod jumped out and grabbed the front fender and the door while Dib steered over to the soft, sandy shoulder. They put some rocks under Mike's front wheels to keep the Lizzie in place. By this time it was pouring rain and impossible to try to find out what the trouble was. They just scrambled into the cab and into their sleeping bags, and put the side curtains up against the water.

At no time on the trip had they felt quite so helpless as they did that night on the pass. There they were, hundreds of miles from civilization, not a living soul for miles, and they were stuck in a car that could start, but couldn't be stopped mechanically. Their car was no longer a champ, at that moment. Dib's journal reads, "We're all cooped up in

Mike after an examination of the heap and a hurried supper."

Just as they were getting settled as comfortably as possible to get some rest after their very long day, a thunderstorm hit them full force, right on the top of the mountain, in their precarious tin car called Mike.

Claps of thunder such as they had never heard in California reverberated everywhere, with long, great fingers of lightning flashing in the incredible darkness. Poor Mike rattled and rocked from the terrific wind, booming thunder, and whipping rain. No sooner would they see a flash and hear a boom than there would be another flash and boom — noise all around them, as if they were right in the middle of the thundercloud itself with the lightning ready to blow all three of them to Kingdom Come.

Since any moment they expected to be hit, it seemed appropriate to get out the bottle of bootleg bourbon Dib's Mom had given them. Under the circumstances they figured she would consider this a medicinal use.

Dib paints Colorado, their fourth state visited, on the back of Mike's cab, while parked on the Rabbit Ears Pass.

Eventually the storm subsided and they did get some sleep, despite the size of Mike's cab and despite the fact that the temperature dropped, in Dib's estimation, to about forty degrees.

Next morning they climbed out of Mike with difficulty, their muscles stiff and sore. The rain had stopped and it was a glorious day. After a good breakfast of bacon and eggs, bread and jam, they felt a lot better and more able to face whatever might be wrong with the Lizzie's brakes.

Their chief concern was that the universal joint was gone. If it was, Mike was finished and would have to be left in the Rockies, and they would have to find some way to get back to California without their car. Tod checked the right rear wheel first, and by turning it could see that the universal was okay because the wheel was free to spin on its axle. Then, with the instinct of a true mechanic, he took off the right wheel completely, just to look around. He discovered that a 2-1/2"-long steel key that secured

Dib stands atop a monument, flowers in one hand and a hat in the other, happy to have made it through the night on Rabbit Ears Pass.

the wheel to the axle had been bounced loose and broken in half. All those rough roads must have been the cause. The wheel would turn, but the axle didn't, and the brakes and gears were useless. Tod remembers, "In those days you were depending on your transmission for stopping. The wheel sheared the key off, so there was no stopping, no gears, no brakes, no anything . . . (If) you're going around a corner, one wheel turns faster than another (and) where you lose one wheel like we did, you have nothing to stop (the car). The hand brake (wouldn't work because it) was a parking brake, and it wouldn't hold on a downhill grade."

The Lizzie's transmission was called "planetary," which meant, apparently, that everything was dependent on everything else revolving in the right way. If any part of the system went haywire, the whole thing seemed to stop working. E. B. White explained it in his famous *New Yorker* article "Farewell My Lovely" a few years later: "The Model T was distinguished from all other makes of cars by the fact that its transmission was of a type known as planetary — which was half metaphysics, half sheer friction. Engineers accepted the word 'planetary' in its epicyclic sense, but I was always conscious that it also meant 'wandering,' 'erratic.' Because of the peculiar nature of this planetary element, there was always, in the Model T, a certain dull rapport between engine and wheels, and even when the car was in a state known as neutral, it trembled with a deep imperative and tended to inch forward."

Tod rummaged through the junk box to see if they could make do with something to use as a key. As luck would have it, the box produced a key that just fit, and all Tod had to do was slip it into the wheel, and Mike had back brakes and drive, and they had back their transportation. So they headed down off the summit east, toward the lights of Broadway once again.

It wasn't until they were riding those restored brakes on hairpin turns that jackknifed their way down from the summit that they realized how lucky they had been to

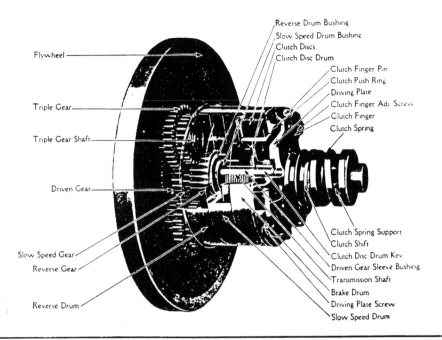

Flywheel —

Triple Gear —

Triple Gear Shaft —

Driven Gear —

Slow Speed Gear —

Reverse Gear —

Reverse Drum —

Reverse Drum Bushing
Slow Speed Drum Bushing
Clutch Discs
Clutch Disc Drum
Clutch Finger Pin
Clutch Push Ring
Driving Plate
Clutch Finger Adj Screw
Clutch Finger
Clutch Spring

Clutch Spring Support
Clutch Shift
Clutch Disc Drum Key
Driven Gear Sleeve Bushing
Transmission Shaft
Brake Drum
Driving Plate Screw
Slow Speed Drum

The Ford Transmission

What is the function of the Transmission? *Answer No. 69*

It is that part of the mechanism of an automobile which lies between the engine shaft and the propeller shaft and by which one is enabled to move at different speeds from the other. It is the speed gear of the car. It sends the car forward at low and high speeds and by it the car is reversed.

What is meant by the term "Planetary Transmission"? *Answer No. 70*

One in which the groups of gears always remain in mesh and revolve around a main axis. The different sets of gears are brought into action by stopping the revolution of the parts which support the gears. By means of bands (similar to brake bands) the rotation of the different parts is stopped. The planetary transmission is the simplest and most direct means of speed control—and is a distinct advantage of the Ford car.

What is the purpose of the Clutch? *Answer No. 71*

If the crank shaft of the engine ran without break straight through to the differential—and through it applied its power direct to the rear wheels—the car would start forward immediately upon the starting of the engine (were it possible to get it started under such conditions). To overcome this difficulty the shaft is divided and by means of the clutch the part of the shaft to which the running engine is delivering its power is enabled to take hold of the unmoving part gradually and start the car without jolt or jar. The forward part of the shaft is referred to as the crank shaft, the rear part as the drive shaft.

How is the Clutch controlled? *Answer No. 72*

By the left pedal at the driver's feet (see Answer No. 9). If the clutch pedal, when pushed forward into slow speed, has a tendency to stick and not to come back readily into high, tighten up the slow speed band as directed in Answer No. 74. Should the machine have an inclination to creep forward when cranking, it indicates that the clutch lever screw which bears on the clutch lever cam has worn, and requires an extra turn to hold the clutch in neutral position. When the clutch is released by pulling back the hand lever the pedal should move forward a distance of 1¾" in passing from high speed to neutral. See that the hub brake shoe and connections are in proper order so that the brake will act sufficiently to prevent the car creeping very far ahead. Also be sure the slow speed band does not bind on account of being adjusted too tight. Don't use a too heavy grade of oil in cold weather, as it will have a tendency to congeal between the

The original manual used questions and answers to explain the workings of the T, in this case the planetary transmission.
From the Model T Owner's Manual, circa 1909.

44

have the brakes snap just where they did. A few feet over the hill, past the easy downslope they had been on, the road descended steeply before climbing to the next pass. In the slippery thunderstorm, without gears or brakes, the three of them, Mike, Tod, and Dib, would have had quite a trip — out over a canyon somewhere, sailing into a steep gorge of the Rockies, gone forever.

Dib automatically edited this possibility out of his letter to his mother. She was already convinced they were starving to death.

CHAPTER SIX

Hard Times

In 1931, 16 percent of the people who wanted to work could not find jobs . . . commercial employment agencies reported 5,000 applicants for every 100 job openings.

— From the chapter "Superfluous People" in *The Invisible Scar* by Caroline Bird

August 18, 1931, found the young travelers camped alongside the Platte River in Denver face to face for the first time with the Depression. Parked next to them were an old man, his wife, four almost grown children, and a granny. The family was living out of a Ford sedan, vintage predating Mike probably, headed for California, if they could make it. They definitely were not pleasure cruising the country, and apparently managed to eat and get along because of the old man's skill at woodcarving animals, which he traded or sold.

It had been two days since their Rabbit Ears Pass experience. The night before, worn out from the storm, they had stopped early to camp beside a creek. They were just sixty-five miles before Denver, if they were to believe a mileage sign they passed. It was a nice enough spot, though, and Dib wrote in his journal, "Went fishing in the evening and Tod caught four darby trout. Had to use worms (as they wouldn't) bite on salmon eggs. I caught 0. We'll try our luck again in the morning. Sleeping in our cots under the

trees." They expected to sleep better than they had in Mike in the storm, but once again were chilled by mountains too high to stay warm, even on an August night. They still had another pass to conquer the next day. In his journal on August 17, 1931, Dib recorded, "Left the stream after a good trout breakfast. Almost all last night we layed awake, freezing to death. After a short run we soon hit Buthond Pass, where the elevation was 11,500." Dib spelled "Berthoud" Pass "Buthond" in his journal and Bertroseld (?) in his letter home. It's not surprising that he misspelled it; so did their atlas, which identified it as "Berthound" Pass. Perhaps in 1931 a lot of people weren't quite sure. "Poor ole Mike climbed gallantly over detours and construction roads. It was plenty steep and we had to use low all the way. Passed through a thunder and lightning storm on the way down."

The dirt almost-road was the steepest they had ever seen, zigzagging from 9,000 to 11,500 feet in about ten miles. To make things even less comfortable, they hit more construction and detours, more dust and pitted roads. Once again the stick was used to jam the left pedal down and hold Mike's low gear in place, and they abandoned the cab and walked beside the car.

Once over Berthoud, our trio coasted most of the miles down to Denver, cutting off Mike's engine entirely when it was safe to conserve gasoline while they drove through yet another Colorado thunderstorm. The hard-worked Model T had burned a lot of fuel climbing the Rockies, and they were both interested in saving money and improving that mileage per gallon average if they could. Later Dib calculated they used 28 gallons of gas from Salt Lake City to Denver, a distance of 560 miles — about 20 miles to the gallon instead of their usual 25 to 30 miles.

The roadsigns were only at a few strategic spots, and not at all abundant in 1931, rare enough for Dib to take this photo. Notice that the sign just identified U.S. 40 with arrows, but doesn't say which way is east or west.

As they entered Denver that afternoon, the Lizzie started making terrible sputtering noises, bucking away like a mule, and then suddenly died altogether. They rolled it to the side of the road and discovered the gas line was clogged.

Not surprising, Dib said. Some of those desert gas stations looked pretty cheesy. Tod agreed, adding that he wasn't so sure about the petcock business and what it was doing to the old car as well. When he loosened the coupling and blew out the line, it cleared immediately, and they were on their way again, into the mile-high city of Denver.

It was not yet 5:00 p.m., early enough to check the General Delivery window at the big white post office and find more letters from home.

Dib wrote that day, "O.K. safe & sound in Denver. We got over the two big obstacles of the journey, Deserts & Rockies. Gee, I wish you could see these Mountains, what monsters. We climbed around & around up as high as 11,500 ft. Plenty high when you look around at the top . . . Gas is 18¢ here. Climate nice & warm. City very good, what we've seen so far. Post Office fine, will write Gert soon. We're good & healthy so don't worry. Fresh food in every town. Hello to rest & Love." He enclosed "Flowers from the exact top of the Rockies."

Now their two immediate concerns, the price of gas and getting warm, were taken care of.

Camp that night was toll-free on the banks of the Platte River. Dib added an "ehem" to the free in his letter, because they weren't supposed to be camping there. Neither were all the other people who were settled along the shore. Some looked as transient as the three of them, but others appeared to be settled for as long as they could manage to stay.

At one location, on the opposite bank, a whole town of makeshift packing crates seemed to be permanently camped — lean-to shanties with strung-out canvas on ropes to create some privacy. Whole families, children, grandparents, in cars as old and decrepit as Mike, in some cases a lot older and more beat up. They were definitely not transcontinental vacationers, as Dib and Tod were. These were displaced farmers, looking for farms . . . or displaced workers, looking for work. The woodcarver was just one of the many disfranchised who was temporarily making Denver his home.

Tod remembers the transient people they met as being not bitter, but very friendly. "People didn't approach us to see what they could get out of us or lift anything. Nobody was like that. And we had many a nice evening, sitting around and talking, and there was no comment well, you have money and why don't we have it, nothing like that. Or why don't you give us this. No begging. They accepted the small lot they had in life."

After supper Dib and Tod spent some more time with the family, asking them how they felt about being uprooted and living as they did. The old man told them he just figured he and his family were hitting on some hard times, and maybe quite a few others were having the same trouble. He didn't much understand why. He didn't blame Hoover, though, like a lot of folks did. He figured it wasn't his fault . . . how could it all be the fault of one man? He figured it was more like a natural disaster, like locusts or a drought or something. And he figured he could always get by. He always had. Although he heard from some people about a man they said could help all the unemployed . . . Roosevelt was his name. And a lot of folks thought he could save the country, given the chance. But who was to know? Nobody had ever helped him yet, except people one to one, and they were always willing to give a hand, if they could. Besides, now that they didn't have an address, they had no vote anyway, so all that politics stuff didn't have much to do with them.

Remembering the man, Tod said, "I saw him roll a cigarette, I guess I was having trouble, and the old guy came up to me and said Oh, I'll roll that cigarette for you, and he rolled it and licked it, twirled it in both hands and handed it to me and Oh, Lord, my stomach did flip flops. I turned green for a few minutes I think. (These people) were all camped out, family and little kids, and all their belongings would be right there. That's all they had. Old car and they would be laying alongside the tent."

The man talked about camps and the Denver police . . . something about tolerating free camps but not wanting any more vagrants sticking around the Platte. Every so often they jostled the campers around a little, just to keep things moving. When it happened, he explained, you just said, real nice, "Yes, sir" and "No, sir" and did as you were told.

When they were back in their own

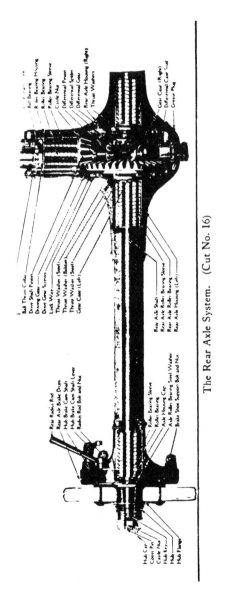

The Rear Axle System. (Cut No. 16)

Chances are that Dib and Tod didn't have the original Model T Manual to go by, but it would have been handy when they fixed Mike.

camp, out of earshot, Dib and Tod discussed their neighbors. Apparently they had a lot to learn about what was going on in their country. These people were real nice, but so different from any they'd ever run into before. Everyone they knew had a kitchen and a place to live, no matter how modest. Sure, Bo and Ed were having trouble finding work this summer, but at least they were living at home, not on the banks of a river.

Dib and Tod were very much protected from the depression. They had money, and a family following their every move. It's ironic that the first place they received extra money was in Denver. Dib's dad slipped $5 (called a "pedro") in his letter. Dib wrote in reply, using a made-up language, "Tod & I emphatically refuse all obnozus and demenstratusermatus denotions from prefisadul part of Eich Liberrdich family. We have plenty & are getting fat. Tod is 183 & I'm 197. Believe it or not." (They actually weighed in at about 150 pounds each.)

In Denver proper, the Model T got noticed in a big way, mostly because of his California license plate. Dib wrote, "What

attention Mike gets, I mean besides us. Everybody turns around & gapes at him. Where ever we (interruption, cops in side car stopped behind us, and we're parked near a side street so I just moved away a couple of blocks & stopped) stop people talk to us & ask us how the good old state is." Everyone was curious about California and their trip and Mike. Apparently most transients in Denver were headed west, to the promised land of California. The three of them were going exactly in the wrong direction, as far as the rest of the travelers were concerned.

That night they set their cots up on the bank of the river. They hadn't been asleep long when Dib felt someone jostle his shoulder. It was a policeman asking them where they were from, where they were going, and how long they intended to stay. Dib was startled and asked if they'd done anything wrong. The officer said they weren't supposed to camp there. Dib started saying something about all the others, when Tod interrupted abruptly, remembering what the old man had said about Yes, sir, No, sir. The cops told them they had a lot of trouble with

Propped up on blocks, broken axle removed, Dib and Tod do work on a major repair in Limon, Colorado.

vagrants, and they'd have to move on the next day.

"Vagrants?" Dib said out loud, but not particularly to Tod. "Vagrants," he said again.

Bright and early next day they did indeed move on . . . at least as far as a park in the city of Denver. It was a big, wooded place with a pretty lake, just their swimming size. They settled by the water to take some sun but some huge blueflies started stinging them. They dashed into the water and escaped to a raft anchored some distance from the bank and the bugs and settled down in the sun. Their last thought at that moment was Mike, and the fact that the car was sitting unattended with all their gear, far from where they could watch it.

Late that afternoon, they swam to

A drain ditch in Limon broke their axle, but town children provided a used one to replace it.

shore, and as Dib got into Mike, tossing his towel in back, he knew right away that something wasn't quite right. He looked around for a minute or two, trying to figure out what was amiss, and finally found it. The old Ingersoll watch, originally gold plated but now worn down to the brass, that had been hanging on a safety pin over the windshield was gone. Someone must have swiped it while they were on the raft.

He and Tod checked the rest of their things, the compartments around the side, the suitcases and such, but nothing else was missing. Ingersoll watches were common. New they only cost about $1.25, and you could take them back and get a replacement within a year if anything went wrong. But used? The watch wasn't worth more than a few cents if you pawned it. If you *could* pawn it. Perhaps a few cents could be very important, they learned in Denver that August 1931.

The bank of the Platte River was their home again that night. This time they chose a spot farther down from where the police had caught them the night before, as the old man had recommended. Technically they *had* moved. No sooner were they settled than the woodcarver came walking over from the next camp, laughing about them being moved along too, saying he hoped the same police didn't show up again that night. They chatted awhile and Dib and Tod promised to buy something from him the next day.

Keeping their word, next day they bought "four jars of jam, 1 jar beets, 2 cans fruit, bar of soap, beans and 2 cucumbers, can of chocolate . . . all for $1.00." (Journal entry, August 19, 1931.) The old man had plenty of trades from his carving and was happy to get the cash.

By midmorning the next day the trio was back on the road, on Highway 40, going east. Denver had been really nice overall, and the police weren't all that mean, but the lights of Broadway beckoned, however dimly, and it was time to move on.

Roads outside Denver were good, well paved and smooth, and they sped along at top speed until another wooden sign let-

50

tered "Detour" appeared along with an arrow directing them off onto an inimproved road.

This was just the first of many detours they hit that day. Despite Mike creeping along at the slowest gait, with detours and sandy roads, they managed to cover the ninety miles to the small town of Limon by 3:00 p.m. It was dusty and hot, and they pulled off onto a side street behind the main town to camp.

Dib was at the wheel, and just as he backed Mike up to turn around, the rear wheels caught in a rain gutter and something went "crack" underneath. He tried to go forward or backward, but Mike wouldn't budge. The T just refused to move in any direction.

The only thing to do was to suspend the old heap on some blocks they "borrowed" from a house nearby, to get a good look at the underside and find out what was wrong. One nice thing about the Model T was its weight. Although it was rugged and designed to take punishment, it wasn't very heavy. One man could easily lift a wheel off

the ground while another placed the blocks under the axle. Once they had the car elevated, Tod tested the back wheels by gently pulling on them. He lifted off the left back wheel and it came off in his hands showing about a six-inch stub of the axle attached. The ditch must have caught it just right to break it.

They both sat down next to the car that was no longer a champ and looked dejectedly at the broken axle. Their junk box contained a lot of things, but a new axle wasn't one of them. Mike looked more than a little absurd propped up on the wood blocks.

Just then some farm kids came skipping and running down the dirt road to get a better look at what was going on in their usually dull small town. Mike and the two Californians certainly livened things up. The old Ford was still loaded with most of their gear, coated with dust from the road. You could read "Mike" on the radiator, but just barely beneath all the bugs. The "New York or Bust" was tauntingly still legible across the cab.

Apparently the children stayed around to keep them company,
and to take a shot of Dib and Tod together while they worked.

About eight children gathered around. Dib remembers, "Just young kids, six, eight years old. And they said what's the trouble, and we tried to tell them what the trouble was. Do you see this? Do you know where we can get one of these things? And they took off and Tod and I continued jacking up and loosening up what had to be done. Probably a half hour, forty-five minutes later the same kids came back and they were dragging a housing axle assembly. They'd gotten it out of a vacant lot. Tod and I weren't too sure about it, but we gave them all the change we had. I think it was seventy-eight or eighty cents in dimes and pennies. Those kids were really happy because they could get an all-day sucker for a penny."

It was too late to work on Mike that night. Instead they walked around the small town of Limon after supper. The town consisted of a few dusty streets, some houses, a couple of stores, and, as luck would have it, a small Ford agency.

Next morning they got up at dawn to start working on the axle, in hopes of beating the flies and the heat. It was eight o'clock when they got started: not early enough, it turned out. The flies were already up as well, and out in force.

The first task, which fell to Dib because he had been driving when the axle broke, was to unbolt the housing, a dusty job that had to be done on the ground, regardless of the numerous flies, heat, and incredible dust. When they were ready to put the replacement housing in, Tod saw that they were probably in for trouble, as the

gears might not match. They were supposed to be the same angle, but one went one way, and the other the other. Mismatched or not, they decided to give the new axle a try. There wasn't much choice.

Tod bolted up the new housing with a gasket Dib bought for three cents from Limon's one and only Ford dealer. He slathered the gears with grease, to help them out, and hoped they would grow to be good friends real soon.

By 1:00 p.m. Mike was back together. The T started and Dib and Tod drove to the outskirts of town to an auto camp. When they got there, Tod hung onto the spare tires in back for leverage and swung under Mike to touch the housing and see how the differential was doing. He pulled his hand right away. It was hotter than a four-alarm fire, but by then they were both tired of worrying about Mike, and the one thing they wanted most was a good shower, to wash off the dust and grease.

To economize they had chosen a spot on the ground, but no sooner were they settled than the sky started rumbling again for miles around, and then enormous drops of water plummeted down on them. It was still afternoon, so they rented a cabin for the night for $1.

Again Colorado displayed her angry side, but this time at least they were not sitting terrified in a metal car. They were stretched out inside a safe, warm wood cabin.

Next morning another warm shower removed the remains of Mike's grease, and they ate a breakfast cooked on a coal stove provided in the cabin. As soon as they were finished, they loaded Mike and thankfully left Limon, Colorado, behind them. Dib called it a "burg" in his journal.

When he wrote home again he automatically neglected to mention their misadventure. His mother was convinced they were both starving and having a terrible trip, anyway, and there was no need to alarm her more. Instead he wrote the things he knew she wanted to hear: "We're in one of the many little towns in Colorado. It's called Limon. I doubt if you'll find it on the map. We're in

The children also photograph Dib and Tod after they finish the axle transplant.

52

an auto camp as we needed a good cleaning up. And are we spick and span. We just finished a big dinner of salad (tomatoes, cucumbers, & flavoring), chili con carne, peaches, bread & cold milk. We're both polluted."

As far as Dib was concerned, his mother never had to know that anything at all was wrong with Mike. But she was darn well going to know they were doing all the things she approved of, like washing and eating good fresh food.

CHAPTER SEVEN

Heat and Flood in Corn Country

Small Town Over Kansas Border — . . . The roads are improving all along. We passed through flat country with corn-fields on both sides as far as you could see. At 4:00 P. M. we crossed into Kansas and parked in a clearing nearly in front of a school. Mike is O.K. now. 4 1/2 gallons (.13 4/10¢ in Kansas)

— Journal entry, August 24, 1931

Dib appeared around the corner of the schoolhouse running as fast as his legs would go after a wily chicken, who just happened to be faster. Tod was standing, football stance, bracing himself with his arms on his legs, panting heavily. "Tackle him!" he managed to gasp.

With that Dib used the last bit of energy he had left to lurch forward and make a grab at the chicken's back feathers. He wound up sprawled on his stomach in the dust, and the chicken disappeared behind the school. He lay there, gasping, for a few minutes, realizing all this driving and lack of exercise were not improving his football game.

The "small town" was Kanorado (although they weren't sure where they were because there was no sign identifying it) right over the border into Kansas from Colorado. Gas was an uneven 13 4/10 cents a gallon, the roads were getting better and better, and the chickens were impossible to catch.

They were driving Mike gingerly, keeping close watch on the heated, mismated axle. It didn't seem to be getting any hotter,

which was a good sign, but stayed as hot as that proverbial four-alarm fire all the time. It appeared the gears were wearing down and grinding themselves in. The metal was fairly soft, and going just thirty and thirty-five miles an hour, it heated up but wasn't really stressed. Eventually, Tod figured, with any luck at all the wrong metal would just wear itself off, and then Mike's gears would mesh and be good for many more rugged or smooth miles.

Tod recalls the axle: "What we did, we matched a pinion. In your differential it is called a pinion gear, a big black gear, it goes against your master. We butted this differential with the ring gear against the master gear, cinched it up tight, put grease on it, and it ran hot — you could fry an egg on that differential the first few days. Oh it got hot! But because parts in those days were different than now, the metal was a little softer. Today with the speed that cars travel at and such, it wouldn't last ten miles. But we were poking along at thirty, thirty-five miles an hour; it heated up, but we weren't really stressing it. The friction wore the metal off so they were just like matched gears."

Our travelers were on Highway 40 and it was smooth going compared to what they had been through so far. Dib wrote to his job-hunting brother Ed on August 24, 1931. "Dear Ed Ole Boy, Hope you've located something when you get this. We're squatted in a clearing in front of the town school. Don't know what town it is, as it's not on the map. Anyway it is in Kansas. Mike sure is a darb, he averaged 20 or more miles per. from S.L. to Denver. Bum roads & plenty Mts. No real trouble as yet. Gas in Kansas is 13 4/10¢ a gal. Pretty low but why the 4/10? Colorado was 18¢. So far all we saw of Kansas was corn, as far as we can see on both sides. The next town is Goodland. Roads are getting better every day (beginning today)."

A back tire had a slow leak but was still usable so they stopped to fix it. A small pinch was causing the leak and needed patching. It was their fourth flat tire in a distance of 1,500 very rough miles. Three hundred seventy-five miles per flat . . . not a bad average, considering the cheesy roads Mike had traveled thus far.

Kansas turned out to be a pleasure to cross, both because of the decent roads and the nice low prices. Dib wrote his family, "Eggs are 14¢ doz. Bread is 8¢ & 9¢. Pork chops are 5¢. They're big too. Potatoes are 18¢ a peck. Milk is 9¢ . . . carrots 6¢ a lb. Pretty cheap all around isn't it."

A gas station attendant told them to head south to hit better roads yet, so at Halford they switched directions and took the connecting State Highway 22 to link up with

Dib sketches the biggest attraction in town besides Mike, in a letter home August 23, 1931.

it. There were two Highway 40s at this point, one called Highway 40N, which wasn't as good as one referred to by Dib in a letter home as Highway 40S. The more southerly route was only seventeen miles distant, running the same direction as the northern route, but following the railroad tracks. Rand McNally labeled it the Union Pacific Highway, Victory Highway, *and* Interstate 340.

Grasshoppers were plentiful in Kansas, forever flying right into Mike's cab through the opened windows. The unemployed were plentiful too. Dib wrote; "You ought to see the unemployed in these towns. They all sit around day and night & just gossip. About 1/4 work and support the other 3/4s." He enclosed a piece of corn. "This is Kansas corn, I think it's going to seed, there's fields of it. I suppose there isn't

An auto camp in Kansas City, complete with a hand pump for washing clothes, and what appears to be a primitive gasoline engine.

any profit so they don't cut it."

They spent the night in a small town of silos and train tracks amid the fields full of corn, overripe and unharvested, in the middle of the flat Kansas prairie. Dib wrote on August 23, 1931, "The two of us are just sitting peacefully in Mike at the end of the main street in Grainfield Kansas. Mike's in the shade of trees, it's about 5 oclock. The sun was plenty warm all day and its still shining. When we first arrived here (about 3:30) we drove around & found a keen place in back of the new school. While I went to the store in town, a janitor told Tod there was no camping but we could finish supper. We had big pork chops, boiled potatoes & carrots, onions fried with the meat, cold milk & canned pears, also bread & jam. Do you still think we're hungry. We eat like that every night." To sleep, they moved to a field right in the heart of the small town, "Just across the street from a traveling circus, all the way from Texas." Dib recalls, "The circus had two open corrals, a tent with some planks for seats, horses, ponies, some clowns, and even a bear."

In the morning a heavy dew was over everything, including their bags and Mike. Dew and cold nights were commonplace to them by now, however, and they didn't feel concerned or worry that Mike might have suffered from the dampness. It was one of their mornings to cook the bacon from home — a little moldy by now, but just as good when they scraped off the mold and sliced the meat underneath. While they busied themselves preparing and setting up the meal, two eggs apiece sizzling in the bacon drippings over the Coleman stove heat, one by one five men came to sit nearby to watch them. One man was slicing a watermelon, and handed out big chunks to his buddies as they joined him on a fence. The travelers felt like a bigger attraction than the circus when the men just sat and stared at them, turning now and again to spit seeds over their shoulders. Tod remembers, "There were these hayseeds sitting out in the field, eating watermelon. Understand that behind the main street meant one store in town — it wasn't

56

that populated, and this was out in the field. They were doing nothing but spending the time of day."

Dib and Tod hurried their meal some and got the cleaning up out of the way faster than usual. When Mike was loaded with their gear, neither the battery nor the crank could start the engine. It would turn over, but without that familiar purr. Tod kept jerking the crank, over and over again, his thumb carefully tucked under, but nothing doing. Mike just wouldn't catch.

Lizzies were famous for being reluctant starters on cold or damp mornings. Being from the moderate climate of California, Dib hadn't had to deal with this cantankerous side of the car most of the time. But this morning it just plain wouldn't cooperate. Tod dried the distributor and tried the crank. Nothing. He dried the wires some more, but Mike still refused to catch. He cleaned the distributor and tested the coil and spark plug wires, still no go. They coaxed the old heap for an hour or more, trying to undo the frost of the night before, while the men just sat and watched, spitting watermelon seeds over their shoulders.

Eventually one tall skinny fellow got up and ambled over to them. When he got up close, he kind of peered into Mike's engine and asked if they had a file. Tod rummaged around in the junk box and quickly came up with a small metal file. The "hayseed" reached into the old Ford's points and

A new friend in Kansas begs for food during breakfast.

gave them a couple swipes with the file. "It'll start now," he said.

Tod cranked and Mike rumbled to a start. Apparently the points had become pitted and weren't opening and closing properly. Filing them removed the burrs, something Tod, as well as he knew Mike, hadn't thought to do. They were quite impressed by the "hayseed." He returned to his buddies and was working on another piece of watermelon, watching the entertaining two slickers as they moved their strange Model T out of Grainfield.

As they drove away, Tod said he'd never seen anyone eat so much watermelon so early in the morning. Dib pointed out that watermelon didn't cost much, if anything, and they were both suddenly aware of the good bacon and egg breakfast and their full stomachs.

Mike chugged along through the flat, seemingly endless plain of middle America ... through Ellis, Hays, Gorham, and other tiny towns that seemed somewhat aloof, certainly alien to anything they'd known in California. The roads were good, the weather sunny, the food cheap, and they kept Mike steady without pushing, letting that axle take its time. It was easy to cover 100 miles a day or so, and to stop early to give all of them a rest. In Gorham they befriended a hungry police dog and would have taken him along for company, too, but Mike's cab just wasn't big enough for three.

The highway followed the rail tracks pretty much and was quite wide and well paved, mostly cement that was straight as an arrow.

In Soloman they slept on the ground in the town park, right next to the railway tracks. When it started to rain, they moved themselves and their sleeping bags into a freight car sitting idly on one of the sidings. It was dry and preferable to the wet ground. They fell asleep soundly, only to be rudely awakened once again that night when the car made a terrible lurch forward. They scrambled down and out just as it started moving away down the track.

Next day they finally got their

chicken. It was crossing the road rather dizzily and Mike hit it square on. When they stopped to pick the scrawny thing up, it just didn't look appetizing enough to keep, so they left it by the road.

In Topeka, Kansas, around August 28 (he lost track of the day for the moment) Dib wrote home, "We're eating Sallie's candy thank her its darby . . . Today is Thurs., Aug 25? We got in about 3 p.m. . . We are staying at an auto camp (35¢) for 2 nights. We had a good shower & shave. Tomorrow we go swimming at the open air swimming tank in the Park (10¢ with suit). It's the biggest public tank in Kansas, we saw it already & it's darby. We'll be carefull - no need to worry. Topeka is a pretty nice town, 20,000 pop. There were quite a few swimming today . . . Mike sure is going A#1 - 4 1/2 gals. used 11¢ a gal. Expensive traveling I don't think. 23 miles a gal."

He apparently needed to address some concerns his mother had and wrote, "There wasn't much traffic on the Mts., except when there was a hold up. Steamshovels & trucks would work for 1/2 hr. then let the line on both sides get by. Both of us got out of 'Mike' & walked up to where the trucks & shovels were & sat down & waited. Otherwise traffic wasn't bad." There must have been some gang shootings in the paper, because he assuaged her fears by writing, "Don't be afraid about gangsters & us. We won't ever see any. That was all talk maybe about N.Y. Even if it is true they'll not look at us." On the eating issue he said, "Don't worry we have more than a side of bacon left. We have other things for breakfast. Pancakes or mush - not always bacon. We always have fruit."

It felt good to be lazy and stop moving for a bit in Topeka. They watched miniature golf at a course named Tom Thumb, an elaborate (if tiny) system of hills and vales, waterways and bridges. Miniature golf had been all the rage in San Francisco, so they

An admirer took Mike's picture on Highway 40 in Kansas and later sent it to Dib's home in California.

were familiar with it. One big building in their home city had been converted into many floors of nothing but miniature courses. In Topeka they didn't play. They were still watching their pennies, and there was still some distance to go to Broadway (and quite some distance back). They even passed up a dance, too, for five cents, and Dib reassured his mother, "I don't think we'll dance. We may watch."

The following day they spent several hours at the municipal pool, swimming, sunning, and eyeing all the pretty girls. Dib wrote home, "Just came back from swimming and finished supper. It's about 5:30 now. We've been in camp about an hour. The swimming was swell, from 11 to 4 we swam or layed in the sun. It's a plenty big outdoor tank, and the water sure felt good . . . Topeka is a pretty city alright. There (are) plenty of parks and trees on the outskirts. Downtown has wide streets. We leave it all tomorrow, Sat., and will be in Kan. City. We'll stay

about 3 days & go to St. Louis for a couple, then north. All we painted on Mike since is the states we went through. He looks like a regular traveler."

They watched miniature golf again, until everyone disappeared to an open-air pavilion with lights all around where a big all-colored band, King Oliver, was making lively music. Dib wrote home, "They dance fox trot & something else, we didn't see any glide. Dances cost 5¢ each."

Next day they were Kansas City bound. Dib wrote home from Kansas City, "Mike sure gets tumbles on the road. People toot their horns & wave as they go by. Most of them turn around for a good look after they pass. When we see Californians, gee, they yell & wave like wild indians. It seems good to see a Calif. license. We see them pretty often too. The other day a car passed & a fellow waved a camera out at us. They stopped a block or so ahead & this fellow got out so we stopped. He wanted a picture

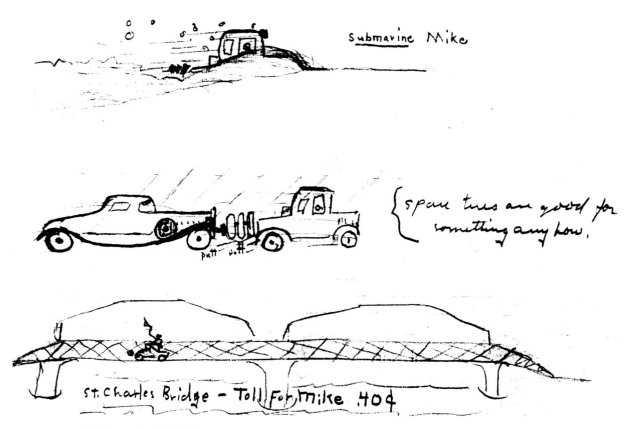

On September 3, Dib drew a wet Mike crossing "St. Michael's River" in the Kansas flood, its rescue by a Packard, and the crossing of the St. Charles bridge over the Missouri River.

of Mike from the rear so we let him take one. He took my address & said he'd send me one. So look out for a letter to me."

To get Mike set up just right, the photographer had them pull the Ford into the middle of Route 40, so it sat diagonally across both lanes. With all the maneuvering and focusing and talking back and forth, it must have taken half an hour of blocking the main highway before they moved on again. Since they were the only cars on the road at the time it didn't matter.

By two o'clock on Saturday, they arrived in Kansas City, just in time to check General Delivery at the post office. There wasn't any mail, but Dib got another package of homemade candy, quite a treat.

They stayed at the American Camp "pretty far from the downtown part" and slept on the hardest, most packed solid ground they had ever run across. The shower was good, though, and there was a horseshoe pit, which they took advantage of to practice throwing. The next day was Sunday, and Sunday in Kansas City they found was just this side of not moving. The city pools were all closed (someone told them the pools were going broke — people just weren't paying to swim anymore). No shows were open, and Tod couldn't buy any tobacco because of the Kansas Blue Law restrictions on what could be sold on Sundays. After wandering around the city in Mike, they finally found a baseball game to watch, then devoted the remainder of the afternoon to trying to locate a more comfortable piece of ground. Dib wrote in his journal, on August 30, 1931, "Later we rode into Missouri looking for a better camp ground. Found none and got disgusted after riding about 50 miles. We returned to the old camp ground, where we ate as usual and sat around carving wood." Whittling wood, just lopping pieces off the ends of sticks to see what might appear, was a common pastime. It apparently didn't matter if they actually made anything; it was more just the activity. It also meant a time of just hanging around, not doing much of anything.

Dib commented on the twin cities again in his September 1 letter. "There are as many bridges between the 2 K.C.'s as up in Seattle but they're dirtier looking. Underneath are freight yards instead of a good River."

Early Monday they checked the post office, but out-of-state mail wasn't sorted until about 1:30, so they poked around Kansas City some. The further they got away from California, the more important mail became to them. Dib wrote, "On the main st. parking is 2 hrs. The cop marked all tires except ours, tourists can park as long as they want. We got tired of K.C. & wouldn't have stayed but we wanted to get mail. That's one of the joys of this trip." Tod wrote a rare letter to Mrs. Fewer. "Dib and myself both got a hair cut in Kansas City Kansas yesterday, and it only cost 25¢. The barber didn't make much money on us, for we both needed a hair cut pretty bad." Tod backed Dib up on how well they were eating and how undisturbed they were even when it rained. "We're all through breakfast now, and what a breakfast, we had cantalope, mush, coffee, bread and jam, in the middle of breakfast it began to rain, but it only lasted a few minutes, so we didn't mind at all."

After the haircuts they checked General Delivery again, expecting a deluge of mail. All there was an airmail letter for Dib from his friend Robin. When they checked the Missouri side, they found five letters from home waiting for them, including one from Pinky with a dollar bill enclosed, in payment of the bet he lost about Mike making it past Denver.

Getting an airmail letter was something. Most mail was sent overland, by train, and cost three cents a letter. Airmail cost five cents and was still quite new. The first official airmail flight was in May 1918, from Washington to New York, and despite the fact that the pilot got lost, it inaugurated regular airmail service. By 1931 it took thirty hours for mail to cross the continent by train. By air, it took about twenty hours, not a big savings in time. The planes could only fly during daylight hours. Dib's letter probably arrived by flying during the day and traveling by train at night.

Another reportedly "first" airmail flight was made on September 23, 1911, and went just nine miles from "Aeroplane Station No. 1, Garden City Estates, N.Y." to the Mineola post office. The pilot was carrying fifty pounds of mail on his lap, and when he couldn't land at Mineola, he tossed out the letters and let them scatter where they would.

It was already getting late when they left town, so they stopped just ten miles east of Kansas City in a field, setting up cots to avoid the multitudes of grasshoppers (and any possible centipedes, like the one Dib spied at dinner). As they fell asleep they could see lightning in the distance. A torrent of rain woke them in the middle of the night, and they headed for the only refuge, Mike, so they wouldn't get soaked.

The lightning and thunder were tremendous, almost a repeat of Rabbit Ears Pass, and they got little sleep that night again. Next day the sky was dark with clouds, the air clammy, heavy with moisture. About one o'clock it began to rain again. And rain, and rain. Dib modestly estimated it was about two inches every half hour, just a slight exaggeration, perhaps. Mike was soaked through but kept chugging ahead through a soggy Missouri.

Dib was at the wheel when they came upon a rain ditch across the highway. He described it: "The concrete road had about 3 inches (of rain) on it all the time. There were two rivers on both sides about 10 feet from the road. Every now & then we would hit a big puddle & spray would fly all over Mike. Pretty soon Mike began hitting on 3 cylinders. Rain was driving down all the time. Well here's the climax or the beginning of the end. We came to an actual river flowing across the road, it was about a block wide. There was nothing to do but go through it. I guess I hit it too fast - about 15 per. & water completely shot over the top. We couldn't see out the windshield as the water was too thick. All I could see was the side of the road. There weren't any other cars in sight so there wasn't any danger of a collision." Dib always anticipated and allayed his

mother's concerns. "Mike began sputtering so I put her in low & used the choke. We just got to the other side of the river when bang, Mike stopped. We knew the ignition was soaked so we hopped out in the pouring rain with the shamy (?) & tire pump & tried to dry the plugs & wires, but as soon as we lifted the hood water just poured in. We couldn't do anything till it stopped raining & that looked like a couple of hours. In about an hour a Calif. license guy asked us what was the matter so we told him & he gave us a push for about a mile. All this time we were watching heaps get stuck and get pushed out of the river. I doubt if the river is still there but I named it St. Michael."

Dib had figured that if he could get Mike going fast enough, full speed or almost full speed, whatever Mike could manage on just three cylinders, the old Ford could make it through the water and onto the other side of the dip. Tod figured they could dry the spark plugs with the air pump, but it was like trying to dry them in the middle of a waterfall. As soon as they got some water off, more water was right there to replace it and form a pool in the pockets around the plugs.

After the push, Mike lasted a little while, but at the first grade just stopped. Once again they tried to dry the spark plugs, but it was useless. They just sat there, waving at passing cars, until finally a big Packard came up to the back of Mike, right up next to the spare tires, and gave them a shove. Dib continued, "This time after a run the ole darb hit on 3. We went a few miles & pulled in the next auto camp. They sure had neat cabins for $1.00. We got the wood stove going and did it get hot. For supper we had a hot XX, soup, steaks, spaghetti, stewed apricots & coffee & bread. I guess we're used to outdoors as we didn't get colds." Dib recalls, "He pushed us at high speed and we swerved back and forth on the slick pavement, but the driver stayed with us until the cylinders one by one came to life. We waved the driver off with a big thanks."

That night at Jay's Auto Camp they finished the last of the bootleg bourbon, and

Tod thought that he might have to agree with his mother that there was the possibilitgy he might never get back to San Francisco again, especially if Dib continued to drive.

CHAPTER EIGHT

Mike Visits Middle America

Toledo is a plenty big city and it looks O.K. to me. We heard from a fellow near the P.O. that the banks went broke and lots of people lost their life savings. He said Toledo was hit the hardest of any city around here.

— Letter to Mrs. Fewer, September 10, 1931, from Michigan

The next day, September 2, 1931, Dib wrote in his journal, "Got up early, ate and cleaned up our cabin. Left around 10:00 A.M. No rain today but cloudy, later on we got a little sun. Saw plenty of rivers and muddy creeks after the rain which was the worst here in three years."

Dib wondered whose idea it had been to dry the spark plug wires with the tire pump, and Tod wondered why he had tried to turn the ditch into the Indianapolis Speedway. Their chamois jackets were definitely hosting a lot of water, despite the exceptionally warm fire in the cabin. (Everyone they knew in San Francisco owned a chamois jacket like theirs, with knitted wool sleeves. They were great for warmth, but not quite the thing for Missouri wet weather.)

Mike's spark plugs had apparently dried out overnight, though because the trusty flivver started with a minimum number of turns, all plugs firing. Tod insisted on driving.

They covered 115 miles that day and by 3:00 p.m. found themselves in St. Louis,

Missouri, "a little ahead of schedule as we didn't expect to be in St. Louis for a few days." Campgrounds were scarce, but they finally found one at Forest Park, "St. Louise's big park. They have a place for tourists. It sure reminds me of Golden Gate Park." The beautiful, well-maintained "tourist" area didn't charge and didn't mind if they stayed all night.

Approaching St. Louis they had crossed a tollgate with a sign posted reading, "St. Charles Bridge, 40 cents," Dib wrote later, " I forgot to tell you from St. Louis we crossed over the Mississippi R. What a big stretch of water & I guess it was narrowest where the bridge crossed. The bridge was a wopper but we couldn't stop to take a picture as trucks etc were behind us." Driving slowly to get a good look, cars started honking at them. They had to move along to keep the traffic flowing. There were no bridges spanning the bay near their homes in San Francisco as yet. The Bay Bridge was to be constructed in 1936, the Golden Gate not until 1937. All the bridges in Missouri, Ohio, and Michigan impressed them because they had never seen the like.

As usual they headed right for the post office, to check for word from home. Nothing there, but they got a good look at the city on the way, and the city got a good look at them. Mike created a stir now, wherever they drove. Not too many overloaded Model T's from California named Mike were wandering around the tree-lined "plenty wide boulevards," and everyone, including the policemen, did a doulble-take when they passed.

Dib called it "St. Louise . . . City of the St." A lady of a city, with policemen on downtown corners directing traffic and keeping everything orderly. Dib wrote in his journal on September 4, "On every corner the cops would say 'Hello', 'Come on Mike' or 'Attaboy Mike,' etc., all of them were good-natured. One lady said, 'My God, from California,' as if it wasn't possible."

St. Louis was peaceful and un-

crowded, their public campground by the river exceptionally pleasant. It was so appealing they stayed three days. Day visitors used the park all the time, although they were practically the only overnight car there. The second night a group of six "machines," as Dib called them, full of young people drove up and parked near them. They spread out their tablecloths and proceeded to barbecue chicken. As soon as Mike was spotted, Dib and Tod heard, "Hey. Look at the car from California!" Three young people came over and admiringly walked around the Ford. They invited Dib and Tod for dinner, but the two had already eaten. "What luck!"

That night was the second without bad weather. They retired early under clear skies, but by 6:00 a.m. it began to rain again. They shuffled their cots under a tree for protection and didn't get very wet this time. Next day they drove all over St. Louis looking for a "tank" for swimming but couldn't find one. They did find a golf course and became spectators for a while, but they really wanted to do something active. Later, back in the park, they played catch with their baseball.

In St. Louis Dib mapped out their trip as far as New York and sketched it for his mom. Earlier he had written, "We won't go to Chicago as they have fast signals & Mike would take a beating." Unless there was a particular reason for going, they wanted to avoid big cities. They projected going to Springfield, Illinois, through Indianapolis, Indiana, Columbus, Ohio, and then north to Toledo, Ohio and Detroit, Michigan, across into Canada and through Toronto, down into Buffalo, New York, due east to Massachusetts, then south to Connecticut and New York.

They left St. Louis about noon the next day, stopping for a mail-call at the post office, and then crossed into Illinois for the first time. For the first time in a while, too, they left Route 40 for Springfield (to pose Mike in front of Lincoln's house although they don't record taking a tour) and took Highway 66.

Mike crossing the Missouri river at the Kansas Citys, going from Kansas to Missouri.

It was only a four-hour trip to Springfield. Dib wrote in his journal, "We left St. Louis behind about noon, after getting some mail at the post office. Traveled steady on highway #66 through green, pretty country. About 4:00 p.m. we pulled into Springfield and as we could not find a place to camp we kept right on going. We turned off a road into a clump of trees behind a church. We ate supper and wrote some letters before we turned in on the ground." They had gone about 115 miles and were in Riverton, Illinois, 7 miles east of Springfield.

The roads in Illinois were basically good, the countryside more picturesque than Missouri — green, rolling hills, little farms and even an occasional split-rail fence. The land looked rich, not at all as if the nation were suffering hard times. They sat high in Mike's cab, surveying country settled earlier than any they had seen yet, reading out loud the Burma Shave signs placed 100 paces apart alongside the road.

"GOLFERS! . . . IF FEWER STROKES

. . . ARE WHAT YOU CRAVE . . . YOU'RE OUT OF THE ROUGH . . . WITH BURMA SHAVE."

And "THOUGH TOUGH . . . AND ROUGH . . . FROM WIND AND WAVE . . . YOUR CHEEK GROWS SLEEK . . . WITH BURMA SHAVE."

And "ARE YOUR WHISKERS . . . WHEN YOU WAKE . . . TOUGHER THAN . . . A TWO-BIT STEAK? . . . TRY BURMA SHAVE."

It was a nice way to tick off the miles. Sometimes they would try to read the signs on the other side of the road, backwards, but that was quite a trick. "BURMA-SHAVE . . . IS THRU . . . THE WAR . . . CHEER UP FACE . . . PARLEY VOO . . . HINKY DINKY."

It helped pass the time.

The farther east they traveled, the inexpensive auto camps gave way to roadside places, well-kept clusters of cabins with whitewashed stones advertising "Kitchens" and other conveniences they could do without. They cost as much as $3 a night, several

A clear picture of Mike in front of Lincoln's home in Springfield, Ill.

days travel on their budget. They had to use their heads and find vacant lots and fields to rest in. The next night they were able to do that and "camped in a field off of the concrete highway" thirty-five miles west of Indianapolis, Indiana.

Mike was running like a champ, the mismated gears blissfully wedded. Detours were few and nothing as rough as any they had seen in Nevada and Colorado, but bad enough. The road surface was pitted and often just dirt. They had hit another thirty-five mile detour somewhere on the border of Illinois and Indiana. "We crossed from Illinois to Indiana about 2:00 p.m. The country is very interesting, but we got 'Flat-tire' Number 5 on a bum road." They had traveled 2,000 miles with only five flat tires, still an exceptional average.

On September 6, 1931, they set out for Indianapolis to take a look at the city famous for auto racing. Dib wrote from an auto camp seven miles east of Richmond, Indiana, "Pretty brisk morning when we got up, the dew was on our bags. We left the hayfield and hit more detours for seventeen miles. Passed through Indianapolis at noon. The stores were all closed because of a holiday. Passed through Richmond about 3:30 p.m. and then into Ohio State. All the way the roads were paved. Had 'Flat-tire' #6 in Richmond. The tires are getting a little ragged." In a letter to his younger brother Bo on September 8, he says, "We went through Indianapolis the city where they have the auto Races. It's just like any other city I guess, we just stopped for grease & gas. Mike is a honey but had #6 flat today. I suppose we'll get a tire pretty soon."

A constant concern in his letters home was Ed and Bo, his two brothers who were looking for work. Another theme was football, thoughts of which occupied a lot of his waking, and sleeping, time. In Topeka he wrote home, "Thanks an awful lot for the papers, it makes my hair tingle to read about what Poly will do this season. We just finished reading the whole bunch. All the fights & football prospects are keen. Tell me when you write how Poly and Decia are doing."

Another place he writes, "Hope Poly conquers, that's about all I dream about is football."

The next day in Columbus, Ohio, the right front tire went flat. It was their seventh flat on the trip, and their average was going way down. Mike limped along to Columbus on a very worn spare tire that had such a big patch they could feel the bump every time it hit the road. It was 3:30, and after checking all over the small town, they finally located a tire they could use at a garage on a back street. Since it was still early, they decided to look for a welder to take care of a leak in one of the rivets near the oil drain plug that had been bothering Tod for some time.

Fixing an oil leak in Mike wasn't going to be easy — if at all possible. Since the oil was in the crankcase, it had to be drained, and it was impossible to separate the welder from the fumes, which might be quite dangerous. They hoped they could find someone willing to try it.

The man who sold the tire directed them to another garage a few blocks away where a man was reluctant to chance the welding. He thought a guy on the next block had one of those new welder tools. At that garage, a young man got under Mike and looked at the leak under the transmission. He said he wouldn't fool with it with an acetylene torch, because he would have to heat the metal red hot and the oil in the transmission would make a lot of smoke . . . might even explode. But, he told them grinning, look what I got the other day. He led them into a cluttered garage and pointed proudly at a metal box that was about three feet square. It was an arc welder, electric at that, and brand new. It should be an easy job and 100 times safer without a flame to fool with.

They pulled Mike in front of the garage and watched as the man slid under the front with his new magic tool and took care of the leak. He charged them $5 for his trouble.

Heading out of Columbus north, toward Toledo, Dib saw a likely place to camp in a schoolyard and they got set up in the recreational field. So far they hadn't had any trouble with the police about camping, except for that one incident in Denver. It seemed that as long as they left the place clean and neat, nobody would mind if they camped almost anywhere. They were seasoned campers by now, able to spot a good place right away. They often chose places other people might not think of, such as church grounds and schoolyards. Wherever there were trees or soft grass, they figured it might be open territory. So far they hadn't had much difficulty, but the more populated the country became, the harder it was to find a place to park. Every few days they would find a cheap auto camp with showers and clean up. Dib wrote on September 10, "Near Springfield we camped beside a church under the trees. Sun. night we camped in a hay field, about 25 miles from Indianapolis. Mon. we camped in an Auto Camp & had two good showers before we left. Boy did they feel good, we're nice & clean now. Tues. night we slept behind a keen school outside Columbus. We were up just in time as the kids came to school. They didn't seem to mind us camping on their school field. Even the Janitor said 'good morning' & talked awhile.

Roads were good in Ohio, but they did hit detours. Even the backroads were sometimes paved, however, and the detours were nothing like Nevada. They still slowed them down, though, and despite an early start, Dib and Tod didn't get to Toledo until 3:00 p. m. . . . just in time to struggle through the busy, congested city to the main post office and find out that they hadn't received any mail.

Dib wrote home, including a "Drawing of Mike crossing a suspension bridge toward Toledo" captioned "Lake Erie" and the comment "(There's plenty of big bridges here)." He wrote, "We saw the first boats since Frisco. Big lake schooners were docked all over. We came in through a couple of bridges and saw the whole works." Driving slowly to get a good look, cars started honking at them. They had to move along to keep the traffic flowing.

Finding a place to camp in Toledo was quite a trick. After driving about ten frustrating miles outside town where nothing looked secluded and everything that did looked private and not trespassable, they found one undeveloped piece of property and drove toward an orchard at the back. No sooner had they unloaded Mike and started dinner than the owner drove up and told them they'd have to move on. He said he didn't mind if they slept closer to the highway, away from the orchard, but he didn't want them staying where they were, and he insisted they leave in the morning.

Dib and Tod reluctantly loaded Mike up again and moved back to the road, as he had suggested, closer to the highway. Dib wrote, "Wed. Night . . . we slept in a real estate tract. We happened to be near an orchard and the owner said we better move out nearer the highway. He was afraid of us going into the orchard." He told Tod crossly the man was probably afraid they would steal his fruit and said it was a pity they had just bought some. Dib wrote in his journal, "What a miserable night last night, mosquitoes by the regiments attacked us. It was plenty hot and we had to keep under cover all night."

The next morning, early enough to miss the disagreeable owner, they headed for Detroit, hometown of the Tin Lizzie.

State road signs in the Midwest were white bands on telephone poles, imprinted in black
– *Courtesy Rand McNally*

CHAPTER NINE

Mike at Highland Park

Drove to Detroit and arrived around 11 A.M. It's a swell city, what we saw, and all concrete roads leading to it. We had to cross a couple more bridges. The signals in this part of the world don't clang when they change and I always wait for a bell. Usually the guy behind us is the bell for me. When we drove into the city we stopped and asked a cop where the P.O. was. He smiled and pointed at a big building on the corner. We were looking right at it and didn't know it.

— Letter to Mrs. Fewer, September 11, 1931

Dib and Tod felt like experts at cross-country travel by the time they reached Detroit. They had gone well over 2,000 miles in their battered up Tin Lizzie, and Mike was running like an old darb for them. The oil leak was sealed, the differential no longer ran hot — the gears quite at home with one another by now. And they were in legendary Detroit, where the Model T and the whole mass-produced car business had begun and matured to the point that a car like Mike assembled in about an hour in 1921 could wind up on the West Coast in Pinky's garage, and even come back again ten years later.

Cars, cars, everywhere, on the streets and in the lots. Dib couldn't believe how low the prices were compared to California. He wrote home on September 11, "Gee how cheap the cars are up here. A brand new Willys Knight Sedan perading (?) around for

$495. What a darb too. You ought to see all the new Fords in Used Car places. All the latest models, 1931 roadsters & coupes etc. $50 to $85 down, complete about $250. They cost $500 to $600 in S.F." Of course they couldn't afford a Willys Knight or a new Model A, bargains or not, but it sure was fun to look and dream. Willys Knight was Dib's favorite car. He recalls, "(It) didn't have any valves (and) there were no moving parts on it. A real quiet engine, (it) didn't make a sound, not a whisper . . . I don't know why they couldn't have used that (engineering) more. Maybe it couldn't go as fast." Other cars were manufactured for reasons other than economy, unlike the Lizzie. The Pierce Arrow was made for looks and performance, with total disregard to price.

Autos were plentiful, but auto camping was not. The first night, after driving around and around in Mike, they finally lo-

70

cated a spot on the Detroit River ten miles east of town. Mike had a tree to sit under, and they had the river to swim in, although it was private property and again "the owner told us to move in the morning." For the second night in a row the mosquitoes ate well on them.

Driving back into town the next day was tricky. Heavy traffic wasn't all that safe for the old Model T. Mike didn't have any of the armor the later cars had, like big bumpers and hefty fenders. As Dib wrote home, driving in Michigan was different than in California. Traffic was heavier and the lights just changed silently from red to green with no bell. Poor Mike received his share of angry horn blasts to get going. In San Francisco all the signals had a bell attached, just in case the drivers weren't paying attention. In Detroit, traffic was more sophisticated, and either more alert or in a bigger hurry. Detroit's first traffic light had been a railroad switch lantern borrowed from the Michigan Central Railroad. It was oil fed. It gave way in short order to a storage battery type, which was considered quite modern.

It was logical that Detroit would have the most up-to-date signals, since that's where the automobile was most at home and in the largest company. In the mid-twenties a native by the name of W. B. Bachman was a pioneer in establishing warnings for motorists. He was the man who came up with the idea of putting a coffin-shaped sign, a full five feet high and two feet wide, at sharp curves to get drivers' attention and slow them down. He also felt it was appropriate to put the admonition "Don't Kill a Child" on signs near schools.

After the policeman directed them to the nearby post office, Dib explained, "Well there wasn't mail yet. (Thurs.) so we bought plenty of eats & inquired for a camping ground & swimming." Nothing was available in town, so they had to head out of the city, south this time, and "finally found this keen place on the river about 15 miles S. of Detroit." It was an idyllic place with shade trees and an easy-sloping riverbank where they could clean up and swim. After a long dip to cool off from the incredibly hot weather, they ate supper and turned in.

Dib takes a look at the Highland Park Ford office in Dearborn, Michigan.

Again the mosquitoes were busy. Buzzzz it. Buzzzz it. They dive bombed their way into the sleeping bags and "ate them alive." It seemed pointless to move, so they weathered the night there. It was some consolation that they could hang around and swim

Some Interesting Figures

The production record of the Ford Motor Company since its organization June 16, 1903, is one of phenomenal growth eclipsing all achievements of the industrial world. Surely such figures could only be made possible through a product so valuable and widely serviceable as to be an almost common necessity:—

In 1903-4, to Sept. 30, there were made and sold.....	1,708 Ford cars;
In 1905, the Company built and sold...............	1,695 Ford cars;
In 1906, there were made and sold a total of........	1,599 Ford cars;
In 1907, the total of cars made and sold was........	8,423 Ford cars;
In 1908, the production and sales reached...........	6,398 Ford cars;
In 1909, the phenomenal growth began with.........	10,607 Ford cars;
In 1910, the production jumped to a total of........	18,664 Ford cars;
In 1911, there were made and sold a total of........	34,528 Ford cars;
In 1912, production more than doubled, with........	78,440 Ford cars;
In 1913, a new high mark was reached with.........	168,220 Ford cars;
1914 saw an even greater triumph achieved by.......	248,307 Ford cars;
While 1915 crowned all efforts with a total of.......	308,213 Ford cars;
In 1916 the volume of production reached..........	533,921 Ford cars;
In 1917 the record was raised to...................	785,432 Ford cars;
For 1918 the estimated production is for............	900,000 Ford cars.

As a more practical illustration of what it means to produce 900,000 Ford cars in one year, and also as an evidence of the buying power of the Ford Motor Company with its "spot cash" payments, the following items speak for economy in manufacturing:

Over 400,000 tons of steel are required for the cars.
126,000,000 square feet of rubber cloth material for tops.
3,600,000 each of wheels and tires.
4,500,000 lamps.
15,884,414 feet of Vanadium steel shafting and axles.
4,938,000 square feet of plate glass for windshields.
109,484,404 feet of copper tubing for the radiators.
12,900,000 pounds of steel for Ford magnetos.
30,838 miles of wiring used in magnetos.
7,836,593 square feet of galvanized metal for gasoline tanks.
55,000 horsepower developed by gas-steam engines and generators.
69,959,951 square feet of sheet metal for guards and fenders.
27,940,382 feet of tubular radius rods.
156,546 freight cars to handle material and product in addition to 79,534,404 pounds of material in less than carload shipments.

Approximately $10,000,000 profits are shared annually with employes.

During 1916, more than 200,000 persons visited the Ford factory at Detroit, and were conducted through the big plant. 1917 will see a large increase, as in the month of August 43,219 visitors, from all sections of the country, paid us the courtesy of coming to see the home of "The Universal Car."

Average number of persons engaged in making and selling Ford cars in 1917 totaled about 100,000—supporting a city of half a million people counting five to the family.

This 1919 Ford sales brochure proudly, if immodestly, points out that the production record of Model T's "eclipses all achievements of the industrial world." It records the phenomenal growth of Ford from fewer than 2,000 cars in 1906 to 900,000 in 1918.
Original pamphlet by Ford Motor Company, circa 1919, courtesy of Polyprint Publishing.

and write letters before they broke camp next day. Dib wrote, "Mike is under some trees & we're sitting in the sun writing. The weather is warm and just cool at night. Most nights its plenty warm. The owner of this place said it was alright to stay last night but to move today. After we have another good (drawing of man diving into lake) as we had a darby time yesterday in the River we will move on. We'll call for mail again . . . when we're leaving as Mike takes a beating going in & out in the traffic. It's too far in the city so will wait till tomorrow." He enclosed some shells from the banks of the river near "Lake Erie," and praised some "Erie fruit, a nice juicy peach. What a flock of them we got for 10¢." Since the Lizzie had had seven flats so far, and as the tires that were on looked pretty worn, they switched the front tires to the back, to even out the worn places. About 2:00 p.m. they broke camp.

Next stop was the Ford factory. Pinky Robinson's mother was going to let Henry Ford know about their trip, but no letter was waiting for them in Detroit telling them what to do or where to go. Dib remembers, "Our neighbor (in San Francisco) realized we were approaching Detroit and she wrote to the Ford factory and told them we were going to arrive . . . Our address was always General Delivery, and so when we were in Waterbury (days later) we got the invite from the Ford Company to come and see them, and they would be glad to visit, but we were already past by far." In an earlier letter Dib had written disloyally, "I hope Henry Ford makes an offer" (but in the same letter he said "Mike is a darling, I'm sure he'll come home with us.")

Highland Park was world famous. It was at this enormous facility that mass production had flourished and the assembly line had been born, all because of the Lizzie. Because Model T's were affordable and so usable, there was an unlimited demand for them. Ford was in the enviable position of having to find a way to meet the demand in the quickest and cheapest way he could. The assembly line began crudely in 1913, when they tried assembling the magneto flywheel with a moving line. Where before it had taken one man about twenty minutes to assemble the magneto, it now took thirteen minutes divided among twenty-nine men. Other parts were upgraded to line assembly, and this quickly became so efficient, parts began piling up at the final assembly point, and it was clear that the chassis itself needed to move. Before the line in 1913 it took twelve and a half man hours to assemble a Model T. By January 1914 four main lines were in motion, all driven by an endless chain, placed at man height so the workers didn't need to stoop, and a Lizzie could be born in the space of one hour and thirty-three minutes.

At the factory Dib and Tod took their own photo of Mike in front of the main office, and then joined a guided tour of the plant. Dib wrote, "What a monstrous place, over 1,120 acres for the whole factory. We saw casting, boring, cutting, molding, nearly the whole works. Of course there are places where visitors aren't allowed. Saw the engines made and put together, also the making of glass. Gee I didn't dream it was so big. Well after that we saw the assembling line. It takes 500 men 45 min. to make a Ford. The belt is over 900 ft., and the car is driven off on its own power. We heard that a new model was coming out. I'll have to tell you about it when I get home. Well I asked the guide if I could get a picture of Mike in the Ford Journal. He was kind of indisposed or bored with us kids, and after the hike around was over he said the photographer went home by now, and come back next week. We were there two nights so we decided not to wait."

Dib recalls the factory: "I Remember Ford's (Model A's) on the assembly line . . . and the place where they had the furnaces for making the glass for their own cars." Tod recalls: "Crankshafts hanging up in what they called humidity rooms — it was all (big) production, but it was very scientific for those days. A very large operation. It took half a day to go through it, just to take the tour. They took you in a bus and you got off at one section and they took you all around and then you got back on the bus, and you got off at another section. A lot of people, maybe fifteen or twenty which was a lot in those days."

New models of cars were still an event, rather than an annual occurrence as became the case in a few years, and the perfection of one model, such as the Model T or Model A, and its reasonable price, was dependent on speed and efficiency of production. If it took only forty-five minutes to assemble a Ford, that meant it cost less in labor, and if the parts were mass produced, that meant it cost less in materials. And costing less all around meant it cost the consumer less on the car lot. As Ford speeded up production, the cost of the Lizzie went down, because Ford passed on the savings to the customer. (At one point Ford promised that if a certain number of T's were sold one year he would give early buyers back $50 . . . and kept his promise.) The first Model T's sold for $850 and went as low as $260 for the Runabout in 1926, a greatly improved vehicle. The advertising slogan read "Ford - High priced quality in a low priced car."

Ford had always had a mind to please the middle class in his country, first by producing cars on a grandiose scale and literally flooding the country and the world with the Model T, and later making the cars bigger, faster, smoother, like all the other companies. By the time Dib and Tod visited the Ford plant, people were already tired of strictly functional designs and wanted a few luxuries, like nicer upholstery, smoother ride, bigger chassis, and such. Of course they weren't *buying* as many, because of the hard times, but that's what they wanted, just like Dib and Tod. When the depression hit, Ford of course was hit, because people couldn't buy as many cars — especially the people he was making them for. The attitude of the day was that big business could save the country, given the opportunity, and Ford made some magnanimous gestures at the beginning of the depression. Despite lagging sales, he raised salaries for his factory workers in an effort to set an example for the rest of the country. Other companies were laying off, and he was keeping his employees and giving them raises. The idea was to have faith in the economy and encourage people to spend, and that in turn would give people more jobs. Unfortunately, it didn't work, and eventually he did have to lay off workers and slow down production like everyone else as the depression deepened.

Hard times hit car manufacturing as well as everything else. Production of automobiles in the U.S. had risen to an all-time high of five million in 1929. By 1930 it had dropped below three million, and by 1931 below two million. That year only four new makes of autos were offered, and none survived. Even so people were always looking for something much better than had been invented before. Dib wrote conspiratorially, "Here's the lowdown. Ford is putting out a new type the 15th of this month." He may have been referring to what was sometimes termed the Model B, a revised version of the Model A that was designed in the fall of 1931 but didn't come out until 1932.

When our travelers finally left Highland, it was quite late and they settled for the night on Coolidge Highway, right near the Ford factory. Away from water, the mosquitoes finally left them alone, and they "had a restful sleep which was disturbed only by a few ants and passing traffic." In the morning they once again visited the Detroit post office, this time rewarded with letters from Dib's father (with another pedro), a friend, Robin, his sisters Gert and Helen, and his mother. "It sure is good to get mail, and how" he told them.

As soon as they had caught up with all the football news they headed out of Detroit toward Canada, wondering if Mike had ever been out of the U.S. before. Tod said for all they knew, the old Ford had been all around the world and back.

CHAPTER TEN

A Night in the Cemetery

WHAT SHOULD BE DONE WHEN THE RADIATOR OVER-
HEATS?   *ANSWER NO. 38*
Keep the radiator full. Don't get alarmed if it boils occasionally
— especially in driving through mud and deep sand and up long
hills in extremely warm weather. Remember that the engine de-
velops the greatest efficiency when the water is heated nearly to
the boiling point. But if there is persistent overheating when the
motor is working under normal conditions — find the cause of
the trouble and remedy it.

— From *The Model T* —
Original Owner's Manual

The car ferry, a big, flat boat with gates at each end, carried them across Lake Erie to Canada. Dib wrote from London, Ontario, Saturday, September 12 (noting that it took four days for mail, Frisco-Detroit): "We are now away up in London, Canada. Good Ole London, 'cherrio ole top.' . . . We paid 30¢ to ferry to Canada & then 122 miles to London on 4-1/4 gals. Gas is 26¢ a gal. here but the gal. is bigger, it really costs about 21¢." He was talking about the Imperial gallon, which is 20% larger than a U.S. gallon. In his journal he says, "the immigrant officers questioned and passed us." Jobs were just as scarce in Canada as they were in the U.S., and visitors were only given three-day passes. Highways in Canada proved to be very good, and they rolled along at record speed. The Canadians seemed very friendly. They laughed a lot at Mike. Dib wrote,

"People are nice and agreeable. Mike sure gets tumbles." Hardly anyone ignored the Lizzie now, whether they were stopped for a signal or getting gas or just driving through a town. Not too many cars from California were passing through Canada either, it seems, and people asked them a lot of questions, mostly about movie stars. Had they seen Clark Gable or Errol Flynn or Bonnie Baker? It didn't seem to matter that San Francisco and Hollywood were several hundred miles apart. Some people asked them about San Francisco's cable cars, which of course they knew a lot about. Dib's dad had been a gripman for eight or nine years, and they were able to testify that a couple times the cable cars did indeed wind up in the Bay. And yes, they did climb straight up the hills, and you did hang onto the outside of them.

Prohibition, signed into law in the U.S.

in 1920 as the Eighteenth Amendment to the Constitution, wasn't in effect in Canada. Dib admitted in his journal that they "had 4.4 beer at a station (20¢ pint)." To his ever anxious mom he wrote, "Beer is advertised but I doubt if we get any. Glad to hear the brewery at home is o.k."

By 1931 everyone who wanted to drink alcohol had learned to obtain it one way or the other, as had Dib's family. Even though his dad was a cop, there didn't seem to be anything wrong with brewing a little beer in the basement. It would only be two years before the Eighteenth Amendment would be repealed, by overwhelming vote, in 1933, and alcohol would once again be legal in most states. Meantime, it was readily available all over the country, from home distilleries, or from bootleggers. Even after repeal, a lot of people went on making their own because it was so much cheaper than the liquor they could buy. Detroit was a center for smuggling illegal XXXX into the U.S. during Prohibition. The very ferry Dib and

Tod took to Canada probably had been used for just that kind of thing, although smaller boats usually went to Canada to pick up the bounty from the thriving Canadian distilleries. In the early days, everyday citizens did the "rum running." They could make as much as $100 a day ($50 per case). That was at a time when Ford was paying a very decent $5 a day for an honest day's work assembling Model T's, and bootlegging became the second largest industry in Detroit, next to the auto industry.

By the end of the twenties, the syndicates had moved in and mobs had taken over. When Dib's and Tod's mothers registered fear about gangsters, they had good reason to be concerned. Gang shootings were common, and they weren't confined to Chicago. St. Louis, Detroit, and New York had their own organized crime "families." In Detroit it was the "purple gang," run by a man named Bernstein who was reputedly exceptionally fond of his mother.

It was 120 miles to London, Ontario,

Mike enters Canada for the first time, the fender still tied up by a cable,
followed on the ferry by a more up-to-date auto.

enough of a trip for one day, and the travelers found a free campground ten miles north of London. It was hot (ninety-eight degrees in the shade, Dib noted), but there weren't any mosquitoes. Next morning it was still hot, and getting hotter when they directed Mike onto the King's Highway headed toward Niagara Falls. At Hamilton, a fair-sized city, they stopped to write letters home. Then they went through Grimsby, Beamsville, Jordon, and on to Niagara Falls and their first glimpse of the water.

Dib reported, "Left our free camp early after a good night's rest. Another hot day. Went on Highway #2 (King's Highway) which was very good. Arrived in Hamilton about 2:00 p.m., and wrote a letter. Came in sight of Niagara Falls around 3:00 p.m. What a sight, the falls are plenty big and noisy. Found a public swimming place and had a swim in the Niagara River. After a good swim, we found a camp sight beside the river."

It was a beautiful, clean spot, apparently bug free. After trying a little cast fishing, without any luck, they turned in for the night on the grass near the car. About 9:00 p.m. it started to rain, so they rolled under Mike to get out of the wet. Because the Lizzie stood so tall, there was plenty of room for them. It wasn't the most pleasant place to be, because Mike's oil had a way of winding up on their bags, but at least it was dry. No sooner were they asleep again than Tod felt something crawl down his neck, then something crawling on his arm, then on his face. He grabbed the flashlight and shined it on the ground to find out that the "things" were spiders. They were everywhere . . . a veritable army. Dib wrote, "We didn't get very wet but what spiders. In the dark they would crawl on our neck and arms. We used the flash and killed about 20 during the night." Tod remembers, "The rain had driven every spider in the whole area who had the same idea we did, to get under the car. We had a flashlight between us and we started killing these crawling things in the dark." There was nothing to do but to climb back into Mike away from the ground. It was still raining in the morning and Dib poetically wrote, "The day dawned gloomy."

Gloomy or not, they took the tour of the falls and the Hydro Electric Power Plant. They'd never seen anything like the power the falling water created, rushing over the rocks and diving straight away into the river, creating a mist that was several yards high. The moisture hung in the air all the way to their vista point. They were impressed with Niagara, and everyone else was impressed with Mike. "Canada" was stenciled in yellow letters on the cab already, and lots of people took pictures of the tourist attraction in the parking lot.

Finally prying Mike away from the curious people, they drove twenty-five miles through the lovely green parks along the Niagara River, across the Peace Bridge (thirty cent toll), and entered New York State for the first time. The immigration officers on the U.S. side shined lights all around to make sure Mike wasn't harboring any illegal liquor.

Dib was not impressed with Buffalo, New York. He wrote, "What a cheesy city, cobble streets in all directions . . . Hunted for hours for a camping ground and then found out that the nearest was 10 miles out on Lake Drive. All cobbles.["Cobbles" made the old Ford shimmy and shake and buck around.] Were we sore.?/#?!!" Apparently

Mike with two admiring darbs in the parking lot at Niagara Falls. Mike drew attention like this throughout the trip.

A first class letter cost 2 cents and as Dib noted, took four days to go from California to Detroit. A postcard cost 1 cent, and air mail was 5 cents. Telegrams, usually for money, were a bit more.

people did not camp in and around the environs of Buffalo. They wound up settling in a deserted yard. In the middle of the night it again started to pour rain. Dib wrote, "Had interrupted sleep, about 12 a.m. it started to rain so we had to leg it across the street and slept on a porch of a vacant house. Very cloudy in the morning; after breakfast we visited the P.O. then left the cheesy joint. How it did pour for an hour. River flowed down the streets. It was wet all day although it rained little. Went through Auburn, Avon and other pretty big cities. Found a camp outside Auburn in a wet looking would-be field." The highways were consistently the best they had ever seen. Some even had four lanes. All the roads, even the secondary ones, looked passable. They were more or less following the old Yellowstone Trail, or Route 5, although there were so many good roads they just chose the ones locals recommended.

Dib wrote home from Syracuse September 16 enclosing some rocks from the Niagara River that apparently tore off a corner of his letter: "They sure have keen highways now, room for 4 cars. They have a series of interstate signs along the highway with jokes, colleges and can you guess the states by their shapes. Some are — ahem." (On the side: "Write soon as we are fast.") One of the lyrics he quoted in part (some of it was lost in the tear) read, "Four & Twenty Yanks, feeling very spry, . . . Went into Canada & bought a case of rhye, . . . the case was

Mike entering Springfield, Massachusetts, nearing the easternmost part of the trip.

opened the Yanks began to sing . . . to our country, but God save the King."

They slept rather soggily outside Auburn, twenty-two miles from Syracuse, New York, and first thing in the morning on the road had their eighth flat tire of the trip. At least the sun was out for a change to shine on them while they patched it. By noon they were in Syracuse, where they got some letters at the post office. Dib wrote, "I hope to see our cousins pretty soon. Mike is still going husky & I reckon we'll get to Conn. alright. It's a keen day here, quite a change from Buffalo." They were headed for Connecticut to visit his mom's sister and family. A few miles later, on the road to Albany, Tod was driving and noticed that something didn't smell quite right. He drove Mike to the side of the highway and saw steam coming from the underside of the radiator. Dib remembers, "It started getting hot and we could smell it, water was coming out of the radiator, a hole in the bottom. We fashioned a wood plug, and drove it into the hole. It didn't hold too good because the radiator was so rusty, but we put water into it and drove to Cherry Valley." Dib explained in his journal that "Mike developed a leak in the radiator and nearly burnt up without water." A hole the size of a half-dollar had appeared, where the drain plug had come loose.

In Cherry Valley, they stopped to have the radiator welded. This time it wasn't a difficult welding job, and they found someone to do it right away. Dib wrote, "The garage man said it would be about $1.50 to fix it. We took it apart & it cost 50¢ to braze the leak." Removing the radiator in a Lizzie was not difficult, but a little time consuming. They had to unhook it from the cylinder head and pull it away from the connecting hoses. It took long enough to delay their camping, and Dib wrote, "After Mike was back together again we got some groceries and found a camp. Ate in the dark."

More rain during the night drove them once again to sleep under the oily Ford, but even with that protection, their bags were soaking wet in the morning. They had to dry off the engine before Mike would turn over.

September 18, 1931, from Westfield, Massachusetts, Dib wrote, "Well here we are folks way out here on the coast. We are in Massachusetts, about 25 miles from Springfield. Tod knows a lady in Springfield so we may rate a home cooked dinner. From there it will be Waterbury, I hope they ask us to stay for the night anyway. Then N.Y. city for a couple of days."

Tired of being wet and dirty, they rented a cabin at an auto camp twenty-five miles from Springfield. The price was supposed to be $1 apiece, but Dib bargained with the lady and they got it for $1.50 for two. After a good hot bath, they slept between sheets that night for the first time since they had left California. Properly cleaned up and rested to approach "society," they headed for Springfield. "Two fellows gave us directions to Tod's friends home. After she invited us to dinner we went into Forest Park to kill time until 6:00 o'clock. A cop showed us the zoo and we talked for 2 hours." Dib's dad, once a gripman, then a fireman, had his own beat as a San Francisco policeman, so there were more stories to exchange. Sgt.

Fewer "walked" the produce and wharf areas in San Francisco.

The wonderful homecooked meal was worth waiting for. Despite Dib's constant reassurance to his mother that they were eating well, it was quite a treat to have everything warm and ready at the same time, and to sit down at a proper table for the first time in weeks. The conversation was good, and they stayed longer than they intended. It was 9:00 p.m. and pitch black when they drove away, headed in the direction of Connecticut, to find a place to sleep the night.

They seldom drove after dark, because Mike's headlights had a tendency to go dimmer when they went slower, not a good feeling when you were charting unknown road. This was another peculiarity of the Lizzie. Tod remembers, "The lights were off the generator, now they're off the battery. They ran off the mag and you were generating your own power so as you slowed down you were generating less power so the lights got real dim." In the best of times, going fast, Mike only produced a low glow.

It was a particularly black night, because of the clouds, and they strained to see if there was any green place they could use

Dib atop a cannon in the city park in Springfield, Mass. In front of the cannon is a more elegant (than Mike) auto, attended by a chauffeur.

Voelkert, Robert

NOT CHECKED OUT

Please check this item out.

for the night. About five miles outside Springfield they found what looked like a park, with no houses around it, so they just pulled Mike in and threw down their bags on the ground to sleep.

Dib wrote in his journal, "A man woke us up by yelling hey fellows, about 6:00 a.m." Tod rubbed his eyes and took a daylight look around. They were surrounded by marble monuments and little vases with flowers in them, as they had spent the night on the well-mown grass of a cemetery. Dib remembers, "The guy yelled at us because there was going to be a funeral, and we had to get out of the way."

He wrote without comment in the journal, "We moved down the highway to cook our breakfast."

CHAPTER ELEVEN

Home Away from Home —
In Waterbury

Dib Fewer and Tod Snedeker, two San Francisco atheletes, have just completed a trip across the continent in a rattle-trap Ford. The trip took them seven weeks and cost them only $90.

— From a Dan Parker column in a New York newspaper,
October, 1931

A twelve-year-old boy came running out of the white frame house at 29 Albion Street in Waterbury, Connecticut. It was Dib's cousin, Frank, and he was just the first relative to recognize and greet them warmly. It was Saturday, September 19, 1931. They were in Waterbury, Connecticut, 3,500 miles from San Francisco, and it was like coming home.

Getting into Waterbury had been a little chancy, as Mike was very low on gas and there wasn't a station in sight. About halfway up a long, steep hill, Mike sputtered and stopped altogether. Because the gas tank was positioned under the front seat, the gas traveled by gravity to the carburetor, which meant that when low on gas and going up a hill, there was the very real possibility that the gas might not make it into the engine. Suspecting the tank was low enough to be almost empty — it was too late to check the level with a stick — they reverted to an

old trick Model T owners used at such times. They turned around, started the engine by rolling downhill, and put it in reverse. The gas tank was higher than the engine and once turned around and backing up, Mike had plenty of fuel. Using every last drop they made it uphill and they stopped at the first station to fill up again.

"We entered Waterbury about noon & found P.O. I got a letter from Detroit here but I expect some more later. A cop told us how to get to Albion St . . . Auntie & cousins expected us. As we drove up the hill looking for #29 a girl was shining a Nash in front of a house. I said to Tod, 'I wonder if that's my cousin.' We turned around & stopped at the curb. A kid ran out and I asked him if he knew me. Sure enough he did, he was Frank, age 12, a keen kid. Kath. age 18, pretty as a picture was the one shining the Nash. She welcomed us & went to tell ma. When we got to the door your dear sis came & was she glad to see us. She kissed me & pulled me in the house. She kept saying, 'all the way from Calif.' 'my what a trip.' She could hardly believe her eyes. She thought I was big also Tod. She sure is a dear . . . Then we saw Denny, 25, Mary, 26, & (Burnie), 21, later. They are all swell. They ask us questions on everything, they think Calif. is the only place to live. We soon ate & talked about Calif., the trip & had to answer plenty questions. Then (Burnie) & a friend of his took us for a ride through Waterbury then to New Haven & Savin Rock."

Everyone was enchanted with Mike. They couldn't believe the car had made it all

Having arrived safely at their second family's home in Waterbury, Conn., Dib and Tod are shown in borrowed suits, with cousins Kay and Mary. Then Kay and cousin Frank pose with Mike.

the way across country, all the way from California. Dad Sullivan, "Mom," and all five Sullivan kids wanted to hear about everything that had happened. They were all rooting for the three of them to make it all the way back to California *after* they had heard the whole story and showed their California kin off to everyone they knew in Waterbury and environs. The travelers hadn't expected quite such a reception.

Dib had never met his Aunt Catherine and Uncle Den before, but his mother had kept her sister and family well informed about their journey. Dib's aunt had immigrated from Ireland in the latter part of the nineteenth century. Her sister, Dib's mom, just sixteen, came not long after, taking a boat all by herself to the East Coast where she stayed some time in Waterbury. She left to join her two brothers, Pat and Den, who were living in California, to work as a legal secretary in San Francisco. Shortly after the San Francisco earthquake and fire in 1906, she met Dib's dad. She hadn't seen her sister since that first and only visit.

Dib and Tod were treated royally to two enormous meals that day, which they ate without shame. Then Burnie, closest to their age, made sure they saw everything in Waterbury that very first night after supper. Yale and New Haven were about thirty-five miles away on Long Island Sound, and a great attraction (everyone had heard of Yale, don't you know) and then to Savin Rock, a concession area where they tried their luck at shooting moving ducks. Tod, the crack shot on the desert with real rabbits, couldn't even win a stuffed one. "After a good time we pulled in at 2:00 a.m. Went to bed between sheets! Something to remember."

It was Sunday when they woke, and Mom Sullivan let them sleep until 10:00 a.m., made sure they were properly fed, and then made sure they were properly escorted to the nearby Catholic church. Dennis loaned his suits, which made Dib and Tod look semi-presentable (although Tod's didn't quite fit). "The church is one of the prettiest I've ever been in," Dib wrote, knowing how happy his mom would be that he was finally inside

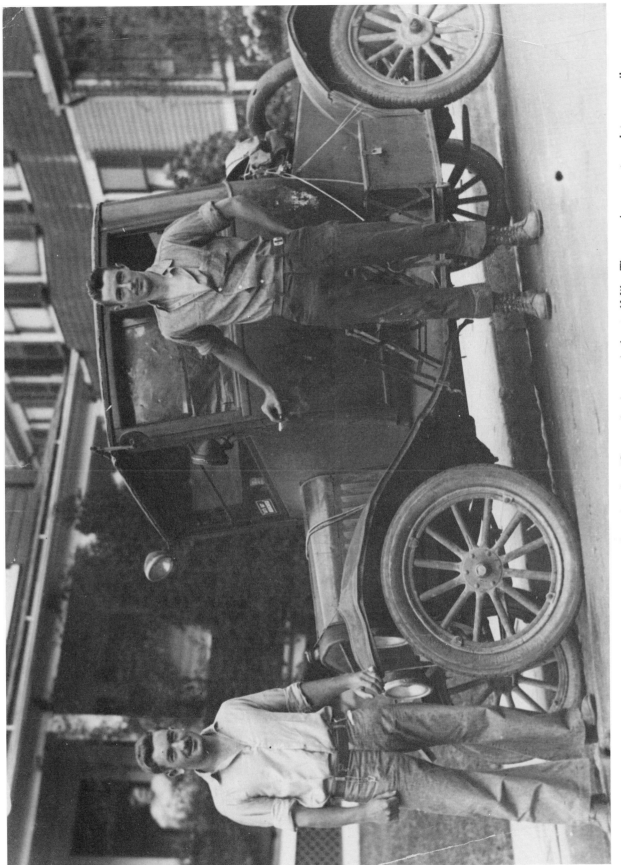

Midway in their journey, Dib (left) and Tod pose for the *Waterbury American* (Connecticut) paper in front of Mike. The camping gear stowed, temporarily, you can see the unpatched hole in the lone spare tire, and a lot of scratches on the celluloid window, which cracked easily and after 2,500 miles was showing considerable wear. Dib sports a pin from a horse blanket, a common keychain of the day, and notice that both young men wear their belt buckles far to the left, which was the fashion.

church again. "As you enter you pay 15¢ at the door & also a collection in side. Auntie gave me a set of rosary beads." Tod dutifully put his fifteen cents in the box, but whispered to Dib that he'd never paid for a seat in his Protestant church. Dib couldn't get over how nice his aunt was. "She's just like an angel, so nice & kind to us. She reminds me of Uncle Pat."

The Sullivan family literally took both of the boys, Protestant and Catholic, into their hearts. There was no question of them leaving before "Mom #2" Sullivan, as Dib came to call her, had made sure they were fortified for the duration of their trip . . . in food, rest, and religion. Despite protests from Dib and Tod about having to leave, she managed to talk them into a few more days . . . and then a few more days, until the days turned into weeks. They attended mass in Waterbury three times before finally saying goodbye (albeit later and later mass each Sunday).

While Mother Sullivan fed them, Burnie and the rest of the cousins entertained them in royal fashion. The Sullivans knew everyone in the small town, and everyone knew about Mike and their trip. They were practically celebrities before they left, quite a new and not unpleasant experience for them. Californians were well thought of anyway, as was California, and the questions never stopped wherever they went, to parties or around town.

Along with being celebrities, which wasn't all that distasteful, they found life to be quite different on the East Coast. For one thing, the men were treated a lot differently. Sunday suppers illustrated this. Tod remembers, "On Sunday they'd all invite their friends home for dinner. The mother would do all the cooking. One Sunday I was there they had lamb, and she'd spent the whole day cutting it up in little cubes cooking it and everything, and then it was put in a pastry about 7" square, the four corners

At Savin Rock, Dib, Tod, Cousin Burnie, and a friend defy Prohibition, at least for the camera, and have a drink.

folded over, and baked, I guess, and then served in a soup plate with this lamb broth. Everyone got their own four or five pies if they could eat them. They were made by the hundreds. But of the whole family, the only ones who sat down to eat were the men. All

Complimentary Football Program

PUBLISHED BY

YALE UNIVERSITY ATHLETIC ASSOCIATION

MAINE vs. YALE

YALE BOWL · SATURDAY · OCTOBER 3, 1931, 2.30 P.M.

PROBABLE LINE-UP

Yale		Maine
20 Flygare	LEFT END	50 Aldrich
40 Wilbur	LEFT TACKLE	64 Kane
55 Tyson	LEFT GUARD	65 Calderwood
43 Doonan	CENTER	66 Fickett
53 Rotan	RIGHT GUARD	53 Buzzell
46 Hall	RIGHT TACKLE	69 Pike
36 Barres	RIGHT END	72 Smith
31 Parker	QUARTER BACK	71 Bagley
48 Booth	LEFT HALF BACK	52 Favor
42 Taylor	RIGHT HALF BACK	22 Sims
49 Muhlfeld	FULL BACK	39 Romansky

SUBSTITUTES

Yale			Maine	
10 Tarlton	26 Lassiter	51 Sargent	14 Wilson	73 Robbins
11 Sullivan	27 MacArthur	52 Converse	17 Lewis	
14 Gould	28 Howland	54 Hawley	28 Frazier	
15 Madden	29 Sandberg		30 Hincks	
16 Holcombe	30 Broaca		34 Riley	
18 Betner	32 Moore		37 Wight	
19 Kilcullen	33 Todd		38 Arnold	
21 Hughes	35 Strange		43 McCabe	
22 Saner	38 Heim		54 Davis	
23 M. Williamson	39 Levering		58 Craig	
24 Inglefinger	44 Crowley		67 Parsons	
25 Ingram	47 Uihlein		70 Hill	

OFFICIALS: Referee, C. L. Bolster, Pittsburgh; Umpire, W. M. Hollenback, Pennsylvania; Linesman, L. A. Greene, Pennsylvania; Field Judge, J. R. Lehecka, Lafayette.

SCHEDULE FOR 1931 SEASON

Oct. 3, Maine	Oct. 31, Dartmouth
Oct. 10, Georgia	Nov. 7, St. Johns of Annapolis
Oct. 17, Chicago at Chicago	Nov. 14, Open
Oct. 24, Army	Nov. 21, Harvard at Cambridge

Nov. 28, Princeton

All games in Bowl except Chicago game at Chicago and Harvard game at Cambridge.

A memorable day at Yale, with the home team defeating Maine, 19-0.

the girls waited on the table. (The men) would stay as long as they wanted, and then when they'd finished, they'd get up and the gals would clear and then they'd sit down to eat."

That first Sunday, when Dib and Tod saw that the women were finished eating, they came in off the porch and offered to do the dishes. Mom Sullivan laughed and told them that men didn't do dishes when there were ladies to do them. Tod remembers, "We felt guilty . . . and insisted. Brian would wash and I'd dry, and then I would wash and he would dry. We'd get out in the kitchen and do it. It was unheard of (and) broke all the rules in the house." Burnie told them they were ruining the whole family, if not the whole town . . . and possibly Connecticut to boot.

To further repay all the hospitality, they played taxi driver with Mike as much as possible, taking family members on errands during the week and escorting Kay back from school — sometimes even to

school if they got up early enough. At night they tried to dance unfamiliar eastern dances like the Connecticut Hop or the more familiar ones like the Irish Jig at parties Burnie took them to. Some nights they just stayed home and listened to the radio — it was something to get New York City — or played cards or just generally played around.

One night they got dressed up and Burnie and Mary took them to a speakeasy — Dib referred to it as a "political meeting" in his journal, supposedly just in case the law got hold of his notes and read where they'd been. Since Prohibition, speakeasies or "blind pigs" were a way of life in many parts of the country, both in big cities and small towns like Waterbury. They were often set up in the basement or an ordinary apartment building, and you had to pass inspection through a peephole to get in. Once inside, the place was usually jumping, often with live music and dancing, certainly with loud conversation and booze. Before Prohibition, respectable women never would be

Mike poses with Aunt Catherine as the Waterbury visit ends, and they leave for the trip home.

caught at a public drinking place. But going to a "private club" somehow made it okay. That's why Mary, in an Irish family that still served the men first on Sunday, accompanied them.

Dib turned twenty in Waterbury on September 21, and for his birthday Kay baked a special cake. The next day the photographer showed up to take their picture. Dib wrote home, "Yesterday we had to get up *early* (9:30) as the photographer was waiting. (Publicity is very annoying) ahem. We were just out of bed when the picture was taken. You'll find the masterpiece on page II. You can see how fat I'm getting. That is your dear Sis on the front porch."

On the twenty-second, Auntie, Kay, Mary, and Burnie took them to see the Marx Brothers acting zany in *Monkey Business* in New Haven. "Gee it sure was good. We sang 'Old Eli' with the Yale students, some class ehwhat." They went swimming in a deserted reservoir, had a haircut (much needed) for thirty-five cents, played cards and partied, but none of these things — not the dancing or flirting with the Connecticut girls or eating Mom Sullivan's food — were as much fun to them as playing and watching football again. Afternoons they would join the local teams at Waterbury Park and play touch football — making passes as good or better than the U.S.C. quarterbacks, and gaining quite a reputation in town for being great California football aces. Despite Dib's getting a painful charlie horse in his leg (which he tried valiantly to ignore and eventually had heat treatments for), they played every chance they got. The Richmond Rattlers would have been proud of them.

Denny worked at the local newspaper at night and was responsible for the photo story on the three travelers. The morning of the interview, they threw on some clothes and posed sleepily in front of the house with Mike, and the photo appeared that evening with most of the information correct. The reporter did get Mike's age wrong, reporting it to be a 1924 model instead of 1921. (Actually, Dib and Tod never were that sure about the exact age.) Dib told

the reporter that Mike was a 1921 Model T with a 1924 engine, and the reporter may just have simplified the facts. When asked how much money they had spent, Dib was embarrassed to tell him how little they had gotten by with, so he kind of hemmed and gulped and said, "$80, maybe $90." The article appeared the next day.

FROM SAN FRANCISCO TO WATERBURY ON $90

Dib Fewer, left, and Tod Snedecker, right, shown with their trusty 1924 model T which carried them from San Francisco, Cal. to Waterbury in seven weeks on $90 including eats, gas, oil and a tire. They are visiting Mr. and Mrs. Denis J. Sullivan, 29 Albion Street, and will soon leave for the coast by way of Florida. Dib Fewer is a first cousin of the Sullivans. The boys hit 14 states enroute and slept under the car during rainy weather. The fenders are wired to the body and the lads have confidence that they will click off their 4,000 mile return journey in record time.

They hit a New York paper a few days later in a column called "The Broadway Bugle" by Dan Parker, who said they were two San Francisco athletes. They like the "athletes" part, and did the best they could to live up to the name.

Football was intensely popular in 1931, all over the country. Young men who could play played it, on local neighborhood teams such as theirs or on school teams. People who couldn't play, watched. People who couldn't watch listened to games Saturday afternoons on the "Flying A," the Associated Oil Company radio program. Competition was keen, and everybody knew all the players on the college teams. Even in California they knew about Albe Booth, a stocky player from Yale who played better halfback than anyone ever had before — or would after, according to reports. He was supposed to run right through the opposition, without them knowing he'd been there. That's why the Sullivans were able to talk

Dib and Tod into staying yet another few days, into October, to catch the Yale-Maine game at the Yale Bowl on Saturday, October 3, 1931. It was quite an event, even if Maine wasn't a real test for the strong Yale team that year, and even if, as it turned out, Albe didn't wind up doing much of his spectacular running. Dib wrote home, "Yesterday we saw Yale play Maine, Eli won 19 to 0. We actually saw Yale, one thing I never thought of as being a reality. Pretty fair crowd in Yale Bowl, but Yale could be taken by Santa Clara."

About the Yale Bowl Dib wrote, "We went inside & it's plenty big but Cal or Stanford is much bigger . . . I signed my name in a tunnel in the Yale Bowl. We rode through the whole campus & saw the different buildings. New Haven is around 35 miles from Waterbury."

While in Waterbury, the letter from Henry Ford got forwarded from General Delivery in Detroit. It was addressed to Messrs Brian Fewer & Tod Snedeker from the Ford Motor Company Engineering Laboratory. Pinky's mom had gotten through to Ford. The letter said to be sure to look them up when they came through. Dib sent back a letter explaining that they had already gone through Detroit and couldn't come back as it was getting close to winter, and as wonderful as Mike was, he wasn't all that warm to travel in. (The letter from Ford disappeared, sad to say, but Brian did keep the envelope.)

Dib was terribly concerned about overstaying his welcome in Waterbury, but his aunt kept insisting that they stay longer. At first she insisted on two weeks, then a little bit longer and then a little bit longer, reluctant to have them leave her safe harbor. On the twenty-second he wrote, "I sure like it here but I hate to impose. They want us to stay 2 weeks or more but we wont." On the twenty-third, "It looks like we'll stay till next Tues. Ten days, you can spank me when I get home. More society tonight. Even though I'm a big shot in the papers, I send my love to you & All." On the twenty-ninth he wrote, "Believe it or not we're still here, I just don't

seem to be able to bust away. We'll surely have to get out this week. Today is Tues. the day I said we'd leave but we are still here for no good reason. Your dear sis just talks until I give in."

A week into their visit, they took one day to drive down to New York City. Manhattan was not a hit. He wrote on the twenty-sixth, "We are now in N.Y. city still in the care of Mary & Kay. Today is Saturday the girls drove us to the big city in the family Chev. sedan. About 90 miles. What a blankety blank city, the worst by far. Traffic & people everywhere."

In another letter he said, "Mary & Kay took us to N.Y. city saturday morning and what a keen time we had. We parked the car outside the busy part & took the subway. Honest the subway is the worst ride I ever had, crowded & no air. It was plenty warm. I wonder how they are in the summer. I suppose they die of the heat. We went into the 'Grand Central Depot', 'Chrysler Building', Empire State, (Largest in World 102 all together), Bronx Park, 'Times Square', also the traffic & subways." The massive city impressed them, though, and so did the traffic. They'd never seen so many cars, all of them fighting to get through the streets first. They were concerned about how Mike would handle all the traffic, but like it or not, the old Ford was going to drive down the length of Broadway. They still had some money riding on it. They ate dinner with some relatives, apparently known to Dib's mom, and then drove the ninety miles back to Waterbury in the Sullivan's car. (It's interesting to note that Mary did the driving.)

Dib finally was able to pry himself away from Mom #2 by insisting that if they didn't leave, the weather would get cold and so would they, even driving south as they intended. In his journal he wrote, "The weather is getting much cooler (had to start the furnace)." He had already made enough apologies by letter to his mother. So on Tuesday, October 6, fortified with practically enough food for the rest of the trip — including a ham, fruit and layer cakes, muffins, crackers, fresh potatoes and celery, ten cans of vegetables, five jars of preserved foods, plus a wool blanket each to keep them warm on autumn nights — they finally tore themselves away from the warmth of 29 Albion Street and were back on the road in Mike. After a tearful farewell, they headed Mike toward New York City and that long-awaited run down Broadway.

CHAPTER TWELVE

New York and They Don't Bust

There is no city in the world that has a greater influence than New York. . . . All over this continent it is imitated, even where it is said to be feared. Men say New York is a warning rather than an example, and then proceed to make it an example.

— A 1931 quote from Thomas Adams, *New York Panorama*, a Federal Writer's Project completed in 1938

As they struggled through the congested streets of New York City looking for the beginning of Broadway, Dib and Tod felt like hicks. New York was a different kind of city, New Yorkers a hurried kind of people.

It was about 2:30 when they arrived and quite a trick to negotiate in Mike. They asked questions about how to get to Times Square, got lost, and generally annoyed New York drivers by not going quite fast enough. People shouted comments at them. "Boy, from California! Look at that!" "Have any trouble with the Indians?" and "How many tires you burn up on the way?" Somehow the comments weren't all that friendly.

Dib wrote, "We were lost for a while but we found Broadway & went all the way up. . . . What traffic, I never saw so many cars going at once." In his journal he wrote, "After a struggle through miles and miles of traffic we found the Post office but there was no mail . . . we rode straight out Broadway. Saw Woolworth, City Hall, 5th Ave., Elevated Trains, Subways and Congestion in general."

"Congestion," it appears, like Mike, had been elevated to a tourist attraction.

The lights of Broadway were glittery, marquees lit up even during the day announcing both movies and live shows. Mike traversed that sophisticated boulevard in 1931, the old Ford's awkward body out of tune with the fantasy, the magic of the theatre district . . . definitely not in place on Fifth Avenue, or even down past the less impressive Battery. Broadway itself, though, hadn't always been so glamorous. There had been a time, before the cement and huge multi-dwelling buildings, when Broadway was a totally different place. *New York Panorama* described the original street as it was centuries before: "Broadway was laid out over an Indian trail that ran along a chain of hills from the Battery to the vicinity of Canal Street, where another trail cut east to Maiginnac, or Corlear's Hook, and west to the Village of Lapinikan, where Indians crossed the forest-fringed Hudson to Hobokan, Hacking and on south to the Delaware. Covered with Oak, hickory and chestnut, the chain of ragged hills extended to Canal Street where valleys and marshland on both sides of the hills spread across the island — so low that at high tide water flowed from river to river. In the valleys and the grassy dales between hills were the log houses and fields of the first settlers. Cowpaths across the marshes gave access to the upper part of the island, precipitous and wild, in whose somber forest and impenetrable thickets of grapevines, creepers, blackberry and raspberry bushes lurked the wolves, foxes, bears and panthers that preyed on the farmers' stock. The plentiful deer and turkeys, too, sometimes destroyed his crops."

Broadway's buried history, beneath the pavement and twentieth-century traffic, perhaps had taken another form, the wolves and foxes preying on different victims. Tammany Hall, a corrupt and corruptable political administration, had control of the city under Mayor James Walker (it would be a couple years before the Republican La Guar-

dia would be able to bulldoze his way past bribed elections and break up the corruption), and gangsters like Lepke, Luciano, and Schulz ran riot, creating their own kind of menace.

The city reflected the hard times of 1931 more than other places they had visited. You could see the depression in the faces of the people. In small towns or out in the prairies, people had family to fall back on, or land, or cheap crops. New York was crueler. There was no relief if you didn't have work, except by some charitable organization that set up soup lines for the destitute. And in a city the size of New York, there was a high concentration of destitute people. As much as seventeen square miles, nearly ten percent of the residential area, was dark slums, and ten of those miles had been condemned for human habitation. That didn't take into account the people who were on the street, trying to live day by day without income. Even the glitzy part of Broadway was feeling the pinch of the economy. An article en-

Dib contemplates war at Annapolis, on a cannon-cum-tank that makes
Mike, far left, look like it's from another century.

titled "These Full Lean years" in *Theatre Arts*, September 1960, describes the depression's impact in that part of town. "Play production in the 1930's shrank, dropping from an average 250 plays a season to about half of that total. Hollywood continued its merciless raids upon the Broadway scene, signing dramatists, actors, directors. Theater building in Manhattan came to an abrupt halt shortly before the decade arrived; there were empty playhouses from ocean to ocean as the great era of touring plays and stock productions began a steady decline; theaters in New York and elsewhere were demolished to make way for parking lots and garages, and many became movie houses. Vaudeville was near starvation (the Palace in New York changed its two-a-day policy in 1932, when it added films, and for much of the Thirties, films were the sole attraction there). Producers went broke, as did the actors (broker than usual), but there were no mass suicides."

In happier times, Dib and Tod might have had a different impression of the city.

As it was, they couldn't wait to leave. The city was just too big and too impersonal to suit them.

It was 4:30 by the time they'd finished their trek and located the main post office. Dib wrote, "Tod went to see about mail while I staid in Mike. What a crowd collected, on all sides giving 'IT' the once over. There was over 50 people inside of 2 minutes. Was I nonchalant - No! They just stared and didn't say anything so all I did was stare back. Just as Tod came back a mad looking cop told me to move on. I guess Mike was obstructing traffic as there wasn't any signs of 'No Parking'."

Dib remembers, "I stood guard on the car because there was a chance we shouldn't be parked there. Anyway a crowd gathered (Tod: They were all over the place when I came out), a gathering of people. There was a big circle on the street and around the car . . . young people as well as old people . . . It was almost a traffic jam because (of the) oddball car."

Tod and Mike pose outside the Midshipmen Quarters at Annapolis.

oct. 15.-Fri. ~~Past~~ Tallahassee
Florida

Dear Pop and Family,

We are still in sunny Florida down amongst the sugar cane, and what have you. Boy the climate is darby. We are parked again in a Pine Forest, its about 8.30 A.M., will be leaving pretty soon.

At present I'm sitting on a log in the sun minus my shirt. There are a lot of dead trees here. They make big cuts in the side of the tree and nail a trough on to catch the Pine pitch. All the trees of any

2
size have gashes and I suppose it weakens the tree after + they fall down. There are plenty of corpse on the ground

They get plenty pitch in the tin cans but the trees are wrecked.

The highways are plenty good, grass growing on both sides and not steep hills.

As we're headed West now the sun comes from the back of Mike and in the evening its in front. Yesterday I sat out on back for about 2 hrs. while Tod drove. The

3
sun sure felt good. Later Tod. got out there.

We've been seeing a lot of sugar cane but the fields have been fenced in. Yesterday I hopped a fence and cut a stalk of it. This leaf in here is sugar cane leaf.

We crossed the Suwanee River also, it looked about the same as any, no better than the Colorado, Mississippi, Niagara, Hudson or Potomac Rivers.

4
We kept going steady yesterday about 25 miles an hr. We went 180 miles on a little less than 7 gallons. Mike is a honey, the only thing that wears out are the tires.

Well Pop how about another one of your classy letters minus the pedro. We got plenty thanks. El Paso I suppose you can write.

How is Mom, Helen, Aunt, Bee + Ed, of course yourself.

Well adios old dark, regards to the force.

Lots of Love Dib + Tod.

Dib writes from Tallahasee, and sketches how pine trees were sapped of pitch.
He was sensitive to how wastefully they were being used.

Dib wrote, "Well we got out of N.Y. by going under the Hudson River by tube to New Jersey, 50¢." Dib recalls, "the tube was lined with shiny, clean-looking tile and the bright lights made them glisten." They were on Interstate 1, the Lincoln Highway (designated by red, white, and blue bands on the utility poles) paralleling the Atlantic seaboard, headed south. About twenty-five miles from New York, they stopped to make dinner, but as soon as they had eaten they hit the highway again. It was raining and they thought to drive beyond the bad weather. They kept on until 9:00 p.m., much later than they usually traveled, finally camping just inside the city limits of Philadelphia in a field. Dib noted that they had traveled 197 miles, and used "9 1/2 gallons (City traffic)." Although he wrote his mother the spot was fine, his journal said that it was a "clamy night's sleep." As it turned out the next day, October 7, 1931, the World Series was going on in Philadelphia. If they thought traffic had been bad in New York and Detroit, it wasn't anything like the traffic they saw that day. They were stuck for two and a half hours without hardly moving. The weather, too, was humid, "clamy," as Dib put it again, not nearly as pleasant as Waterbury.

The 1931 World Series, was being held

Pennies versus Costly Delays

 You will be surprised at the low cost of getting things done quickly by telegraph. For instance, a Night Message of 10 words can be sent from coast to coast for 60c. The average cost of all forms of telegrams is only 69c.

Even to London, the cost of a message by CABLE is as low as 3 to 7 cents a word. Call our office for the rate to any point on land or sea.

Form 73

Receipt for Telegraphic Money Order

OCT 14 19

Received from Mrs E Teuver

Twenty Five Dollars, to be paid

to Brian Teuver at Jacksonville Fla

subject to the terms and conditions of the Money Order Service.

THE WESTERN UNION TELEGRAPH COMPANY

Charges Paid $2.56

Low cost, maybe, but Western Union charges for wiring $25 to Dib and Tod were $2.56.

at Shibe Park and was a contest between the St. Louis Cardinals and the "World Champion" Philadelphia Athletics. Burleigh Grimes pitched so well for the Cardinals that his team won the series for the first time since 1926. Dib and Tod must have hit the traffic going to the game, rather than coming from, as it was still early in the day when they passed through Philly.

The next day or two they stayed pretty much on historic Route 1, hitting some detours, but traveling through fabulous country they'd studied in school. Outside Baltimore, Maryland, they stayed at an "honor camp . . .pay as your purse allows." Their purse allowed them to pay fifteen cents, and they put that amount in the box at the exit next morning. Dib wrote in his journal, "We got in Baltimore around 11:00 a.m. and I drove to the dock where I was last year. Saw places I knew. [Dib's last port of call as a 'wiper' on the S.S. Wilkeeno freighter had been Baltimore.] Continued to Annapolis and went through the Academy. The next stop

was Washington, D.C. We went around the whole city and saw the Capitol, White House and went up into the Washington Monument (555 ft.) Got mail and an invitation to supper from Mary Wilder (a friend of the family). Saw her too late so we continued out of Wash. on #1 highway. Crossed the Potomac River to Virginia. It rained to beat the band from 6 til 9. When it stopped, we stopped. No supper tonight. Plan to sleep in Mike. Just turned off road alongside a gas station and stopped." They were about thirty miles south of Washington, D.C., in Virginia.

In a letter home on October 9, "writing . . . standing up, my desk is Mike's fender" Dib finally had to ask his mom to send more of their money. She had enclosed a $5 bill in a letter he received in Waterbury, but they were still short: "Will you send $20 to Dallas, Texas by money order or mail. May wire before then."

Finding their way through eastern cities was quite a chore. Mike wasn't at all safe in the stop and go, bumper to bumper

Mike in front of the Jacksonville, Florida, Western Union, waiting for a telegram with cash.

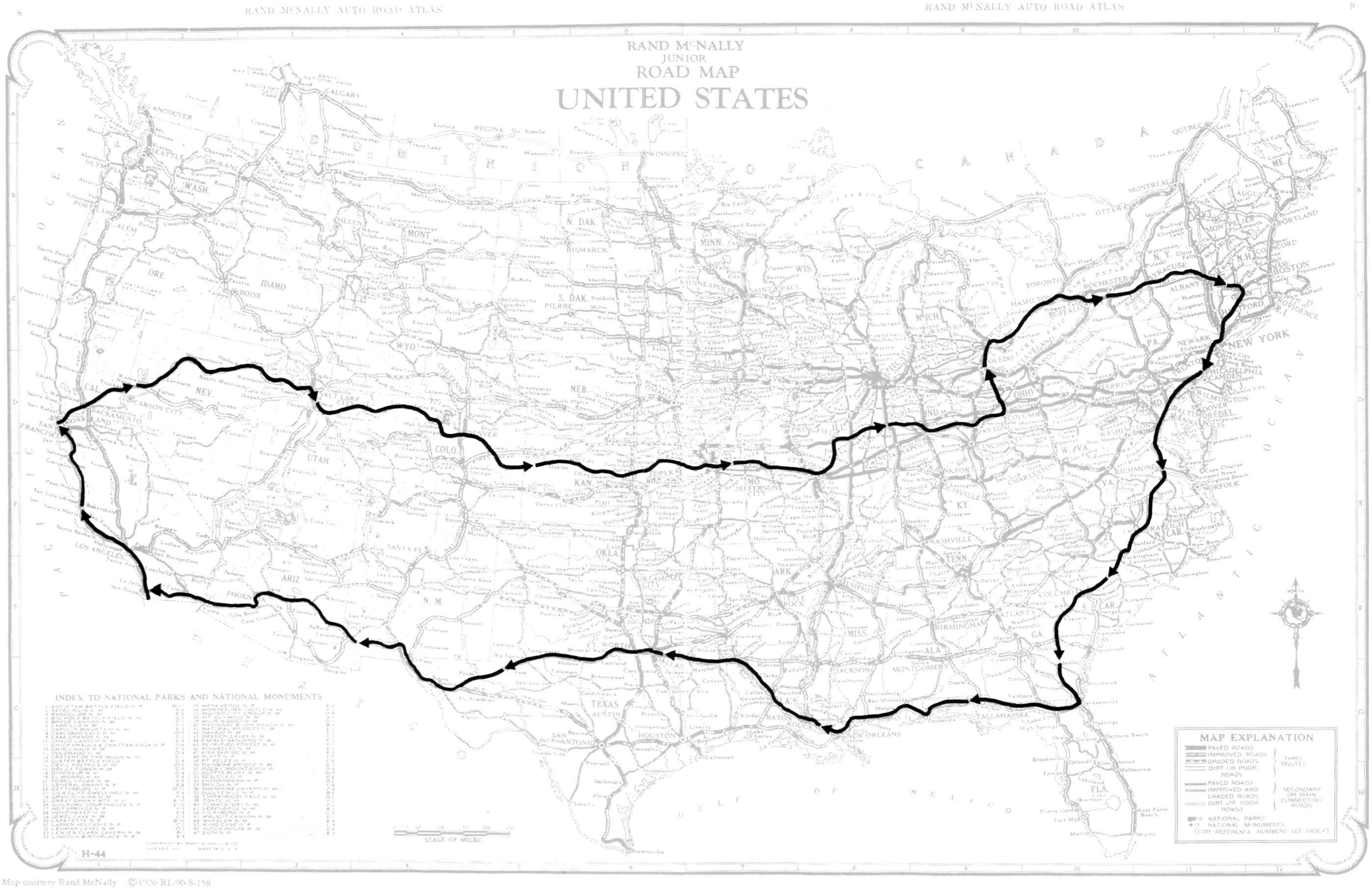

RAND McNALLY AUTO ROAD ATLAS
RAND McNALLY
JUNIOR
ROAD MAP
UNITED STATES
MAP EXPLANATION
INDEX TO NATIONAL PARKS AND NATIONAL MONUMENTS
SCALE OF MILES
H-44

Map courtesy Rand McNally ©1926 RL-90-S-158

downtown traffic. A streetcar grazed the T in Baltimore on the driver's side. The highways weren't clearly marked through the cities, which made it hard to find their way out, once they were in. Most of Highway No. 1 was very good surface and wide. Outside Richmond, Virginia, their ninth flat tire was a blowout so bad they were forced to buy a new one. Not even the patching would work on it. Dib wrote home, "Yesterday, south of Richmond we had No. 9 flat. One of the new tires from Hyman Bros. blew out. Both have been showing canvas after 4 thousand miles. In Petersburg I got 2 new Dunlops for $7.05. So Mike has new shoes and is ready for the bum roads in Ala, Georgia and Miss. We saw tobacco wharehouses for Lucky Strikes & Sir Walter Raleigh. All this country is famous for Civil & Revolutionary Wars. There are old southern mansions and negroes homes all over. In N. Carolina we came into today are plenty of cotton fields. A lot of cotton is going to waste so we got some. Gas is 17 and 19¢ & up. Mike is sure a Lovey, not a knock or miss in her. Still gets 20 to 25 miles a gal."

The receipt from Dunlop Tire and Rubber Company showed that Mr. Fewer of San Francisco had purchased two 30 x 3 -1/2 Std. csgs at 4.70 each, less second tire 1/2 price for a total of $7.05. It was dated October 9, 1931. The weather was getting exceptionally warm and nice, which appealed to them after all the rain. They got a real taste for the South. Dib wrote home, "Boy the weather is glorious, no foolin', not a cloud in the sky. It's about 4:30 & supper is cooking. Potatoes, stewed peaches, peas, tomatoes, bread and Auntie's swell fruit cake . . . The weather couldn't be better here and the highways are all concrete. . . . All through Virginia was swell scenery, green trees and hills on both sides. Everybody speaks with a Southern droll. All give darling Mike the twice over."

Because it got less congested the farther south they went, it was easier to find campsites. The roads were pretty good too — very few detours, and some stretches of "crushed rock in asphalt."

The U.S., indeed, was still experimenting with roads in 1931. A book published that year in England called *The Story of the Road* said of U.S. highways: "In large parts of the Mississippi Valley there is no available road stone and the roads have been made of burnt clay and sometimes of wheat straw mixed with clay. In Florida a mixture of sand and pine needles has been found satisfactory — in the absence of better material; its main disadvantage is that it is inflammable and the roads are apt to catch fire." The very best road for years had been considered to be the "macadam" road, a "weight-balanced" crushed stone road prescribed by John Loudon McAdam in his "Remarks (A Observation) on the Present System of Roadmaking," published in England in the early nineteenth century. Stone had to be broken up to the right consistency and redistributed, with a certain curve at the sides. The first such road was built in the U.S. in 1823, the Boonsboro Turnpike between Hagerstown and Boonsboro, Maryland. In 1931 macadam road was still considered very good, now with a surface that was often oiled. With the advent of cement, things were greatly improved. Dib and Tod were familiar with cement slab road, because outside San Francisco there was a lot of it, in sections as big as could be poured. No tar was spread on top, and cars would bump at each "seam" between slabs. But it was still uncommon enough for Dib to note in his journal when they found cement highway. Early cement roads were often just laid over the land, as Huey Long did in his native Louisiana, without too much thought to engineering. That notorious politician, for all his faults, was a pioneer in road building and financing. By 1931, Governor Long had built more than 2,000 miles of roads, using bonds secured by gasoline tax money. He also used a lot of unemployed men, which made him even more politically popular. (Later President Roosevelt used some of the same ideas to build roads and create jobs across the nation.)

In Raleigh, North Carolina, they got mail and had Mike checked in a gas station.

Of South Carolina and Georgia Dib wrote, "The highway is plenty good through small forests and fields. We saw the darkies picking cotton. Today we saw the first Cotton Ginery. Paid 50¢ toll on a bridge over the river. The water was bright red from the clay."

They had never seen so many negroes. Dib wrote, "There are more darkies than whites." An impressive number of flivvers were still around. "Nine out of ten cars here are Model T Fords." Mike was right at home. They hardly saw any California license plates, though, so the Lizzie was still in a class all by itself, attracting approving attention wherever they went. "Calif. cars are very rare, saw about 2 since N.Y."

They continued on Route 1, burning up the miles. On October 13 Dib wrote in his journal, "Mike is perking 100%, but the new tires are showing some wear already." To his family he wrote, "All through the south are plenty colored people, cotton & tobacco fields, mules and rickety wagons, old shacks and some good looking white girls. The highways are as good as Calif. The scenery is Pine tree forests, fields and small towns. Gas is 20¢ a gal . . . We've passed through the following cities. I guess you still follow Mike on the map. From Philadelphia, to Baltimore, Annapolis, Wash. D.C., Richmond, Raleigh, Columbia, Swainsboro & now Jacksonville."

Because the weather was so good, they had devised a way to keep up their tans — something young San Franciscan football players were particularly interested in doing in 1931. It was easy to open the only door on Mike that worked, on the passenger side. It hinged front to back, and could be left open while driving along. One of them would climb out on to the turtleback back and bask in the sun, while the other drove. Dib described it to his mom, using a drawing to illustrate. "The weather is swell, nice and sunny during the day. We take turns sitting on our bread box with the door open taking sun baths. Its darby . . . No danger of falling. Notice the pockets are still handy."

It was pleasant to sit or stand out back and feel the scenery all around and the sun warming their bodies. Golden fields of tobacco and white cotton fields, little clumps of pine forest that looked inviting for camping. "The trees are small and not thick. The pine needles are neat for our bags to lay on." The road sometimes crossed rivers that had no bridges, and ferryboats carried the three of them to the other side — sometimes free, sometimes for as much as fifty cents. In Baxley, Georgia, they stopped again in a pine forest to sleep. Next day they headed for Florida and traveled through green, forested, flat country across the St. Mary's River into Jacksonville. They entered Florida with the grand sum of $2.50.

It was time to tap the reserve at home more urgently, so they composed a telegram to Mom Fewer. Here's what they came up with for $1.20, collect:

"DEAR MOTHER GREETINGS FROM JACKSONVILLE FLORIDA. WIRE TWENTY BUCKS PRONTO - DIB"

It was 6:00 a.m. California time when they sent the request, so they had to wait until the San Francisco office opened to deliver the wire. They wandered around Jacksonville, waiting for the reply, got a haircut for twenty-five cents, and got noticed in a big way. "A flock of people stood around Mike." By 5:30 they had received a money order for $25 and the message "DEAR BRIAN DELIGHTED TO HEAR FROM YOU LOVE."

Dib's reply by mail was a little warmer than his telegraph request: "We are still in our camp 10 miles W. of Jacksonville. I want to thank you Mom for the do ray me. We don't need 25 but it won't go to waste. I hope you take all expenses out of our sock, be sure & do that. The country is keen and so are the 3 of us."

They were just over a week away from Waterbury, Connecticut.

CHAPTER THIRTEEN

All About Pistachios

It was someplace down in that area this old mammy came up to us, wanted to know do you fix anything. She had some old clock that she wanted us to fix. I don't know why, but I guess we came that far she thought we could fix something. We didn't, though.

— Tod remembering Louisiana

The South was interesting. They were traveling the Old Spanish Trail now, identified by red, white, yellow, and black lettered signs. It was also called U.S. 90 and State Highway 1.

Signs were still in the process of being made uniform in 1931, and they were not totally consistent across the country. It had only been in 1925 that the American Joint Board of State and Federal Highways had been formed, giving the highways new numbers instead of the old named ones. In many places poles and fences still bore the old colored marks, and trails like the Old Spanish Trail were still identified in many spots. Most of the signage was put up by local automobile clubs in the mid and late twenties, since they were the most interested in seeing that their members got from one place to another with reasonable accuracy. Interstate signs were in the shape of a shield and just identified the route, not whether you were going south or north. Mileage signs were just kind of arbitrarily placed. That's why Dib would write, "about 30 miles South

of Washington" to describe where they camped. Occasionally they would run across a sign that told them how far it was to New York or San Francisco (they photographed one of these in Colorado because it was so unusual).

Warning or caution signs were few (although there were plenty of hastily lettered "detour" signs on their way). New York had been the very first state to put up signs of warning. That was in 1903, and they were blue and white and told slow-moving traffic to keep near the curb. In 1924 many engineers felt that "curve ahead" signs shouldn't tell which direction the curve went, because then the motorist would have to go slower until he found out.

At first signs were square, because that was the easiest way to cut them. Then they sawed off the ends to make a diamond shape. And finally they sawed the corners off the diamond. Stop signs across the country were yellow for a long time, although everyone had agreed to use red, only because they couldn't find a red paint that held up outdoors. The exception was in California, where a porcelain enamel red stop sign was used. The very first stop sign, not signal, was put up in Detroit in 1914.

Dib never mentioned lines painted on the road, but they were around in 1931. Those rare four-lane highways he remarked on in New York State probably had lines dividing the lanes. The first painted lines on a street or highway were reported in Redlands, California, in 1912. The first reflective lines for night driving weren't used until 1938 in Minneapolis; it was tape just laid on the road (and it peeled off rather quickly in bad weather).

From Jacksonville the travelers headed due west, the most direct route they could follow back to California. They drove fast now, covering as much territory as they could before that money in the sock ran out.

They were eating well, or at least communicating that to Dib's mom. Mom #2 had given them a big supply of food, and they bought things as they went along. (The bacon was still usable, if moldy.) Prices were cheap, and the food good. Dib noted the "whoppers of bread" that came in big whole loaves, not sliced, so they could cut off big hunks to eat. He recalls, "Tod liked coffee so much he used to buy something with . . . chickery. We tried to go the most reasonable way possible and it was about eighteen cents a pound or something. It was . . . so bitter you couldn't drink it. In the southern states if you got the real cheap coffee it (always)

had (this) chickory in it." Camping spots were comfortable and plentiful, the going easy. On October 15 near Tallahassee Dib noted, "There was not much traffic when we started. The sun came out plenty hot so we took turns riding out on back of Mike in the sun. We crossed the Swanee River about 1:00 p.m." ("Looked about the same as any, no better than the Colorado, Mississippi, Niagara, Hudson or Potomac Rivers" he wrote his dad later, jaded now with all his river experiences.) "Went through Lake City, Live Oak, Montecella and Tallahassee. We got some groceries and found a campsite five miles out of the capitol."

He described their camp: "At present I'm sitting on a log in the sun minus my shirt. There are lots of dead trees here. They (men) make big cuts in the side of the trees and nail a trough on to catch the Pine pitch. All the trees of any size have gashes and I suppose it weakens the tree after and they fall down. There are plenty of corpses on the ground. They get plenty of pitch in the tin cans but the trees are wrecked." Of the roads he said, "The highways are plenty good, grass growing on both sides and not steep hills. As we're headed West now the sun comes from the back of Mike and in the evening its in front. Yesterday I sat out on back for about 2 hrs. while Tod drove. The sun sure felt good. Later Tod got out there. We've been seeing a lot of sugar cane but the fields have been fenced in. Yesterday I hopped a fence and cut a stalk of it. This leaf (he enclosed a sugar cane leaf) in here is sugar cane leaf."

Mike's tires were really showing the miles. On October 16 Dib noted, "Changed the tires as one side wears more than the other. The new tires are going fast." They were really speeding now. "We hit the highway early and passed through Quincy, Marianna, Shipley and other small towns. There were plenty of swamps and forests all along. Saw the lumber mills, cotton fields, cane sugar and farms." To his dad he praised Mike. "We kept going steady about 25 miles an hr. We went 180 miles on a little less than 7 gallons. Mike is a honey, the only things

Outside a tobacco plant in Virginia, Dib sits in Mike in front of a Lucky Strike cigarette billboard.

that wear out are the tires." Gas cost twenty and twenty-one cents a gallon. They camped that night twenty-five miles from Pensacola, Florida, beside the road. After a chilly sleep, they broke camp early and started what was to be an expensive day . . . and a most unpleasant two days and night.

It was in Mississippi that they decided to take home a souvenir, and Dib wrote in his journal that they had "hocked some signs." He remembers: "They were signs that had been knocked down so we borrowed them as souvenirs . . . A Mississippi interstate was one, just the metal shield. We unbolted it from the broken wooden pole." It read: "Miss. U.S. 90" in black print on white.

Dib wrote home, "Well Fri. we were in Florida & made camp in a woods 20 miles from Pensacola. When we went into the city the next day I suggested a swim in the Gulf of Mexico would be good. The only beach anyone could get to was the Pensacola Beach by bridge. The price for us on the bridge was $.75 so we didn't have a swim. We kept going and soon crossed into Alabama. We hit a 10 mile stretch of clay road but it was

smooth so it was alright. We crossed a toll bridge ($1.10) over part of the Miss. Gulf. It is all water and islands here. There would be a bridge then 5 miles of land then another bridge, etc. It was getting kinda late so we started looking for a camp sight. Crossed another toll bridge for .50¢. On the other side we saw a keen place so we drew up on the grass. Before I even stopped 50,000 mosquitoes poured in the sides. Gee I couldn't get Mike out fast enough. As we had just uppers on we got some bites and how. (Uppers were strap type undershirts.) Ten miles later we turned into a field, the same thing as before. I never saw so many mosquitoes before. Boy did they hurt. We had sweaters on by now. It's all swamp land down near the Gulf. A ditch on both sides of the road had water in it. We tried once more and gave up, there were millions everywhere. All the houses are screened and some have a pot smoking on the front porch to keep them away. Hardly anybody is out at night. Those who are, walk with a branch of pine needles and keep swating their faces. Its been like this for 7 weeks they say. The

Somewhere in Florida, road deserted and not too fancy, pines in background.

people are waiting for rain or a cold spell to chase the pests away. Good ole Frisco with its flies.

"Well, we couldn't stop so we kept going into small towns and out again. Very few people could be seen. We drove along the (Mississippi) shore, it sure was a pretty sight. The water was different colors and there were launches & yaughts at anchor. There were swell homes opposite the water. I guess the Van Dusens & Van Derbilts lived there. Well we just kept following No. 61 highway till about 10 o'clock. It was cooler & I thought the pests would be in bed by now so we turned off into a field. They were there alright but only about 10,000 this time. We got out the bags quick and crawled in. What a night of misery. We both got down to the bottom & closed the entrance tight. We got up early Sun. morning hoping they were gone, but no, they kept biting. A Southern gentleman came along all bundled up swating his face with Pine needles. He said it was the worst he has seen them. They stay out all day even in the hot sun. The only thing we could do was start breakfast. The breakfast was the steaks we bought for the night before but didn't eat. We ate while the mosquitoes ate, both having a lovely time heh heh. Tod had his shamoise on and I had a towel on my head. . . . Got in New Orleans

about 11 o'clock. We went up & down the main street. Its a pretty nice looking city. Crossed more bridges. Gas is 14¢ & 17¢. Mike still is a honey. The tire we got in Ohio is finished, just wore out. From New Orleans we went to Baton Rouge where we took a ferry & crossed to where we are now."

Dib remembers: "This delta area was lots of water, we'd cross bridges and take barges across, and some . . . for free and some . . . for pay. It was the main road. We stopped and gee (there) was nice, nice green grass alongside this water and it's terrific. (But then) forty million mosquitoes attacked us. We thought, this is temporary, but it wasn't. We got back in the Ford, no windows, mosquitoes coming in like crazy . . . and we tried progressively, every twenty miles (at a) nice place, but (an) untold (number of times) we couldn't stop. They'd kill you. So we drove and drove and I guess it was about 2 o'clock in the morning we finally got to stop. We had to stop because we were getting whipped, couldn't stay awake."

Because they were anxious to avoid the mosquitoes, they breezed through New Orleans, not even bothering to locate Bourbon Street. Tod remembers, "Of course this was before DDT. In those days they had three or four weeks of this (mosquito weather), they told us, every year. But this had gone

In the Delta country of Louisiana they crossed a portion of the Mississippi River.

on for about (seven) weeks. So when we got to New Orleans we just kept on going . . . Hello, Goodbye." Dib adds, "At that time there weren't all the chemicals to fight insects we have now. They used to spray oil on water for mosquitoes to kill them, but there were too many bayous and still water places there to do that."

Roads on the other side of New Orleans weren't very good — country rather depressed with lots of shanty homes and towns, but the weather was warm and pleasant enough. They "hit some bum road and had flat tire #10. All around there was nothing but Negroe homes and towns. The weather was keen. Got into Baton Rouge about 5:00 p.m. and couldn't find #71 highway." (Actually they wanted No. 61, which might account for why it was so difficult to find.) "At last we found the ferry (25¢)." It was a rickety old ferry with about thirty other cars on it. They "crossed the Mississippi River. Hit some more gravel roads. Found a

camp at crossroads and no mosquitoes." That was on October 18.

They had literally outrun the mosquitoes getting through the swamps of Florida and Louisiana. It was twelve days since Waterbury, and they had covered over 1,900 miles and used 84 gallons of gasoline. After a cold sleep near the Mississippi River across from Baton Rouge (the dew was "thick on our bags") they left and started a fifty mile stretch of gravel road, crossing the Red River on a free barge. Mike was low on gas and stalled completely going up a steep road, so they turned around and backed to the nearest station. Gas was a low thirteen to seventeen cents a gallon in this country. The weather was wonderful, and they sunbathed again that day, eventually stopping to camp twenty miles on the other side of Alexandria, Louisiana, in a beautiful grove of trees they couldn't identify, apparently privately cultivated and owned. The owner, an "old guy" in his sixties, came over to their campsite and sat with them for a while telling them about the South and about pistachio nuts and how they were going to be the thing of the future. He called them "boys" and told them how that grove they were camped in could be a real producer . . . make a lot of money someday, probably. He might just be interested in selling them part of it, if they were interested in the pistachio business.

As they only had about $12 between them, they decided not to invest in their future right then.

Tod tries to keep the mosquitoes in Louisiana at bay by putting a towel on his head and wearing his chamois jacket, despite the heat.

A barge and a tugboat ferry them across the Red River in Louisiana on the main highway.

The travelers stop long enough to take a picture, and then hurry through mosquito-infested New Orleans.
Mike's tires are looking pretty seedy about now.

CHAPTER FOURTEEN

On the Spanish Trail

Of course everyone felt cheered today because the U.S. Postoffice Department announced that the 15 per cent increase in mail indicated better times are coming, probably overlooking the fact that most of those letters are from people writing home for money.

— Clipping from a column by Pat Frayne in a San Francisco newspaper, 1931. Sent to Dib by Mrs. Fewer

In the middle of the night near the pistachio grove in Alexandria, Louisiana, Tod was awakened by a grunting and snorting like he had never heard before. Kind of an "umph, umph, umph." He jostled Dib awake and they saw some hazy forms nearby, messing around in the dirt right at the foot of their bags. It was early, just before dawn, and as they were a distance away from Mike and the .22s, they just kept still until sunup.

Straining to see what was creating those horrible sounds, they finally made out some good sized, about 100-pound, animals that looked suspiciously like pigs, rooting around in the mossy ground for pistachios that continually fell from the trees. Neither of them wanted to mess with wild pigs, so they quietly got out of their bags and got dressed. As soon as they did, the pigs moved to another part of the grove to look for more fallen nuts.

Dib remembers, "They were going through to pick up the nuts. Wildish, though. They belonged to somebody. We were kind of leery of them, and found out later we should have been. They get pretty vicious if for some reason you disturb them."

The owner joined them again while they ate breakfast. He was a chatty fellow, full of stories about the Ku Klux Klan. He told them they should believe those stories they'd heard, because those boys had a lot of power down south and they knew it. A different place than up north or out west. Murders going on all the time, but nobody gets caught. Not like the movies. Since they had turned down his offer to buy the pistachio grove, he asked them if they were interested in buried treasure. He said he knew where they could find a fortune in silver or gold, if they'd stop long enough to do it.

They declined the riches and left later than usual to hit the road again to keep "going steady." A little way along they stopped at a field to get some sugar cane (it tasted strange to them, not sweet like expected). It was a glorious, sunny day, so they took turns sunbathing on the back of Mike.

To get some exercise, Dib ran ahead of the old Ford for a time. It was level and easy going.

The travelers were on Route 71 heading away from the Gulf Coast and into Texas, on the way to Dallas. Route 71 had been called the Jefferson Davis Highway a few years back. Just outside Shreveport Mike started acting funny, losing power and not running well. When the T lost power completely and died they rolled it to the closest overnight accommodations. The place happened to be called Bliss Auto Camp, and was it a beauty, with hot showers and soft green grass to sleep on. Problems or no, they decided to shower before seeing to why Mike wasn't moving anymore.

All cleaned up, they took a look and soon discovered the generator they'd put in before leaving had burned out. When they replaced the original Model T ignition with a Delco, they had also added a new generator to replace the tricky magneto. Tod rummaged around in the junk box and came up with a compact generator to take the old one's place. It was a lot simpler to fix than the magneto would have been.

Tod remembers, "When you burn out your generator, naturally you don't have any juice for spark plugs or lights or anything. No battery. But we did have a spare generator in the junk box — along with the key for the axle and a few other things. We had a lot of essential parts. In those days generators

were four or five inches round. Ordinarily a Model T didn't have a generator, but when we converted to a Delco ignition, then you had to have a generator to supply the juice."

Next morning they entered Texas, the Lone Star State, for the first time. As soon as they crossed the state line the roads deteriorated again. They traveled 150 miles on bumpy and sandy gravel that was hard to maneuver. Dib's journal entry on the twenty-first was: "What lousy roads we hit as soon as we came into Texas. We passed through a couple crowded oil towns — seemed like the gold rush days. Had #11 blow-out on a small stretch of good road. More awful roads — gravel, bumpy and sandy. We have a weak tire on now!" They had been forced to use one of the not-very-dependable spares strapped on Mike's back for emergencies. "We have to get a couple more tires for Mike, he's very hard on shoes . . . . We got a tire with 2 boots on now."

On the twenty-first they found a "nifty camp site in front of an old lodge. A farmer came and talked to us for a while. Slept on the ground." As elsewhere in the South, the people were friendly, and the farmer came to keep them company and praise Texas after dinner. By now homesick, they told him California was pretty fine and they couldn't imagine Texas being *that* good, but they hadn't seen enough to make a comparison yet. (In letters home they kept saying how much better California was and things like, "Home will look good now.")

Next day they drove as far as Dallas — just about fifty miles. "It's a plenty big city, and we finally found the post office and got a flock of mail." They received two letters forwarded from Raleigh "with a pack of letters of the whole U.S. & Canada." Inside one of the letters was a five cent airmail stamp for Dib to "rush a letter . . . of our next address." He used the stamp right away. They only had $9 left and desperately needed new tires for Mike, but it was time to clean up again and stay in an auto camp. Rain was on the way, and they couldn't face another wet sleep, or a cramped night in Mike. Tod wrote another rare letter to Mrs. Fewer

The Southwest was full of towns like this one, Monahan, Texas, that had few people and fewer cars, so Mike was photographed in the middle of the street.

and diplomatically said, "The weather sure has been keen in these southern states nice and hot all the time. It has just begun to rain tonight for the first time since we left Washington, D.C. but we don't mind it at all for we are staying at an Auto Camp here in Dallas, and it can rain all it wants tonight and it won't bother our sleep at all. We have the swellest little cabin that we have had on the whole trip. A nice little gas stove and running water, and a big double bed. Mike the Old Darb sure had been going swell the last few days, the only things that wear out on him is tires, but as long as that is all we don't mind at all. We still get about twenty five miles to a gal." Dib didn't note down how much the camp cost. But he did say they spent some time talking to three fellows headed for Mexico City. Two of them, Max and Rudy, were from Germany, traveling on motorcyles. (Months later they ran into these two in San Francisco, where they settled for a time. The four of them went to several wild parties together.) They also met a Dr. Gauldin, a jolly fellow who thought they were quite the rogues. He apparently said he would give them a dollar apiece if

they wrote him from California. (They did, but not until Christmas, and he said by then the "statute of limitations" had run its course and didn't send the money.)

It poured rain all night, and although they were rested and dry in the morning, Mike wasn't. The Lizzie was completely flooded, spark plugs so wet it took an hour of cranking to get the engine to turn over. Once started, they headed for a post office to see if any more mail and or money might have arrived. No pedro was waiting for them, so for ninety cents they wired, "DEAR MOTHER GREETINGS FROM DALLAS WIRE THIRTY BUCKS PRONTO DIB." Mike needed new shoes. While waiting for the do-rey-me for three hours they "walked all over the city of Dallas and window shopped."

A couple hours later a $30 money order arrived with the message, "DEAR BRIAN SORRY IF MIKE IS MISBEHAVING WRITE LOADS OF LOVE MAMA." Apparently she didn't believe that Dib was telling the whole truth about Mike all the time and thought he needed money for repairs.

Later he wrote his father, "We left

A tanned Dib breaks camp in Texas while Tod snaps his picture.
They have acquired heavier blankets, courtesy of Dib's aunt.

Dallas after dear Mom. sent the money. First we got 2 tires gas, oil, rearend greased, grease in fan & water pump and water in the battery. Mike is in perfect shape so no one should worry about us. We're both feeling hunky dory.

"When we were parked on Main St waiting for the cazoomy plenty of guys stopped and talked to us. Boy they sure think the Ford is a wonder. . . In the Western Union office the fellow asked what kind of car I drove. I told him a Ford coupe. 'What's the car's name.' Gee I looked at him & wondered how he knew (it had a name). I told him Mike. You ought to see him & the lady laugh. She said that Ford has been making history hasn't it. I said sure. Finally found out they got the info from Frisco (from) the money order."

An invoice from Trinity Tire Company, Dallas, Texas, dated 10/23/31 showed they purchased 2 30 x 3-1/2 tires for $9 and had a tube patched for $1. By the time they left Trinity and Dallas, it was already 3:30,

so they didn't go far. The perfect camping spot appeared at some school grounds ten miles from Ft. Worth, Texas. Dib recorded, "As it was Friday and there is no school on Saturdays we stopped at this school just east of Ft. Worth. Had a swell moonlight night and it took some time to fall asleep." They stayed awake and talked about the trip and their going home.

Next day they drove through Ft. Worth at about 10:00 a.m. and gave it a quick once-over. Dib reported "Its a pretty big city, but not as big as Dallas. We traveled over rolling country with plenty of small trees, shrubs and cactus growing all around. Sun was hot all day. We went through plenty of small towns and found a camp about 4:30 p.m. and then ate our supper. We sat in the sun and got tumbles from every car that passed. We slept on our cots." They were twenty miles east of Abilene, Texas.

Texas had grown on them by now. The highway was mostly "improved," not great but "fair" and "paved." Next day they

On the Texas prairie, they have acquired a steer's skull, shown on the back of Mike.

went through a lot more tiny towns over pretty fair highway . . . saw their first Mexican colonies, real cowboys, and some oil fields. A penny postcard to Dib's sister Helen reported, "Texas seems to stretch for miles. Leaving Dallas it looked flat for hundreds of miles but there are some hills. Mike gallops right over them all. We see lots of towns, cactus, longhorns & cowboys." Soon he loved the wide-open spaces and couldn't praise Texas enough. In another letter he wrote, "Honestly Texas is a <u>divine</u> state. Wild & wooly and wide open. Whenever I get a 2 months vacation I'm coming back to Texas. Gee it's wonderful country, not to live in exactly but so very different for a change. It seems more interesting and exciting down here. Nevada was just dead in comparison.

There are small towns every 10 miles about & they (the populace) sure are interested in Mike. Around the border are mostly adobe homes, all one story and just made from adobe bricks. Some are made classy with a little plaster on the outside. . . . Well the sun shines bright & nice & hot every day. Honest the ranges and blue hills and everything make you feel so free, I kinda hate to leave the place. I never thought I would enjoy Texas so much."

They were able to use the .22s again, and one night shot a jackrabbit. It was hard to tell whose shot caught it, so they shared the responsibility. "We went hunting and both of us shot a Jack Rabbit. We later skinned and cleaned him." In a letter Dib elaborated, "We had the same rabbit for din-

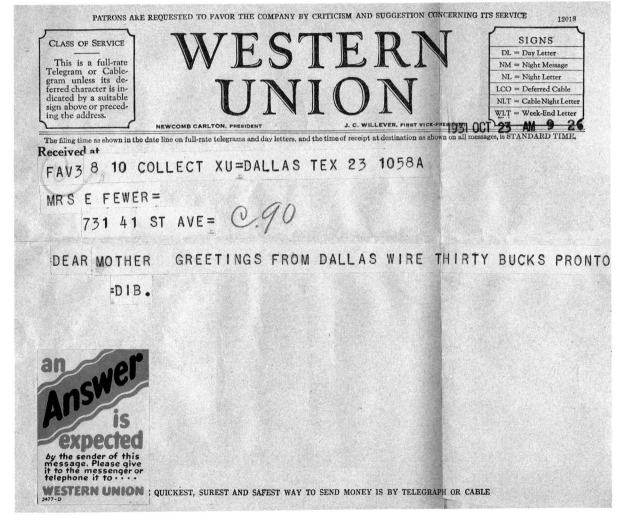

Heading for home, Dib sends an SOS from Dallas for money to buy new tires and other necessities.

ner that night and while we were eating supper a flock of (desert) quail drifted by. We got the gats (guns) & were after them quick. As my gun is cockeyed & shoots a mile high I got 0. Tod got 3. I would aim low as heck but the bullit whizzed into the ground 2 yards in back of them. They finally ran too far for us. When we got back the applesauce we had on had caught (was burning) but not bad. We finished our peaches & cleaned the quail. After all was ready (dark by now) we started out in Mike in the moonlight. It was swell. Nobody around & bright as day. We even drove with out lights in the full moon light." Of the quail Dib remembers, "They didn't fly or hurry away. We followed them and even the noise of the guns didn't seem to bother them. They finally wandered off into the desert protected by evening dusk."

The full or almost full moon stayed with them through Texas. The roads weren't particularly good, but gas was cheap — as little as eight cents a gallon. Top price about seventeen cents. On Monday, October 26, Dib wrote, "While in Texas we've seen lots of Mexicans in small towns. Some of the towns are nice looking with wide streets & big buildings. The highways are fair although they're paived. Gas is from 8¢ up to 17¢. We usually get 12¢. The real cheap gas makes Mike have a spark knock when climbing hills."

They took advantage of the Texas sun to sunbathe on Mike's turtleback and took runs in front of the car whenever they felt like getting some exercise.

From Ft. Worth they followed the Southern National Highway to Abilene, where they picked up Interstate 80 (called Bankhead Highway) to El Paso. It was a long haul from Abilene to the New Mexico border, but the roads were fair, the going easy. They went by Sweetwater, Big Springs, Odessa, Pecos, and Sierra Blanca, but also "hit a small town about every ten miles." October 26 they spent a freezing night "next to a corral in a range just after the town of Van Horn."

Mike was mostly okay, but had been "sputtering every now & then for the last week or so. We knew the gas line or carby was dirty." They stopped in El Paso on the border of New Mexico and "finally took the carby's screen & cleaned it & gas line, does Mike purk now." Dib reported, "El Paso is a swell city and what mail we got . . . . Adobe houses and Mexicans are prominent."

They hadn't been using their spark plug whistle . . . Mike got enough attention without it . . . but the whistle was still attached. Tod recalls how he had installed it. "The spark plug was above the whistle. The whistle screwed in where the spark plug went and the spark plug went over that, in between the spark plug and the piston. The gusto coming out of the whistle was from the piston. It took a little power away from the car, because the spark plug was above the whistle and not where it was supposed to be, down in the chamber burning gas. It was a girl catcher!"

For some reason the whistle went haywire in El Paso and started whining, all on its own. A highway officer stopped them. Dib remembers, "We went down a long drive and then we started coming up and I don't know what happened to the whistle . . . it was making a whine but we hadn't pulled it open. Maybe it crept open in the heat." The cop was "laughing too much" to give them a ticket, but he asked them to cut the noise. Tod had to disconnect the whistle completely to get it to stop. The valve had gotten warped in their travels. (They fixed it a little later.)

This wasn't the only time the law had been involved in Mike's whistle. A few years earlier when Dib was up at the Russian River having a nice time tooting at the girls a cop had stopped him. He let Dib go but said if he ever saw him doing it again, he would give him a ticket. Well, the next weekend Charlie Weaver was up at the river in Ike, having a grand time blowing his spark plug whistle at all the girls. The same cop appeared and let Charlie know he wasn't happy about seeing him again. Charlie tried his best to explain that Ike was a different car, but the cop wouldn't hear of it. He was convinced Ike was really Mike and gave Charlie a ticket.

The spark plug whistle wasn't the only annoying contraption a T could be rigged with off the spark plugs. Some practical jokers liked to run a spare coil from the hot terminal, and shock anyone who touched the car — or anyone who touched the driver — whenever they pushed a button. Another annoyance could be rigged by putting a piece of soft rubber tubing about an inch in diameter and several inches long with a squashed end over the exhaust that would produce a satisfying "raspberry" sound when the engine was revved. For some reason Dib and Tod hadn't fixed Mike up with these extras.

CHAPTER FIFTEEN

All the Way Home

Well we must eat so I'll stop.
Luck to the Rattlers.
Hope Ed makes more $.
Hope Bo gets a job.
Pa - we still have bacon

— Letter, October 30, 1931

By the time they crossed into New Mexico, they were getting anxious to get to California. The days were sunny, the nights cold. They felt free as birds and safe too, although Mrs. Fewer found something besides food to worry about while they were traveling the Southwest. In the North she'd been worried about gangsters and in Texas she was apparently worried about highwaymen and accidents. Dib, as usual, reassured her. "Gee what the heck are you worrying about us getting held up or in an accident. Don't be silly, the brakes are good & I can lick any 2 highway men in the country. (What conceit.)" He must have been feeling powerful from the moon and all the hunting.

The young adventurers were traveling as far south in the U.S. as you could go, just about, across the tip of New Mexico, through Las Cruces, Lordsburg, Safford, Arizona and into Phoenix. They headed through the mountains, where Dib wrote, "We saw Coolidge's Dam, what a honey it is, way out in the plains. The Lake is plenty pretty. We

saw it from altitude & it was nice & blue. We ate at the top of the Mt. & then continued down. The sun was just over the top & what pretty colors it made on the sheer sides of the cliffs. It was really keen, I felt like going up the top again just to come down again. We went through a tunnel cut right through a rock wall. The tunnel was about 100 ft. long. It was a swell ride. We continued & journeyed by moonlight til about 9 o'clock. we pulled off the road into a field that used to have corn in it. Had a real comfortable sleep." That night they made a bonfire and by the bright light of the burning sage bush painted a skeleton steer's head with horns they had found on the prairie and mounted it on the back of Mike. The Lizzie really looked like an old warrior now.

On October 29 Dib wrote from their camp spot fifteen miles east of Phoenix describing the trip across New Mexico. "Mike is hard to start after the cold nights. We finally started on a good highway but we soon hit thirty-five miles of real cheesy road. What bumping and jarring — Poor Mike — we rode through rolling hills and then high mountains. We had to use low gear pretty often. We saw plenty of tree cactus. On the top of the mountains we ate supper and then continued down in the dusk, was it pretty! We stopped about 9:00 p.m. and turned off the highway in a cornfield, to camp." About the Southwest he said, "It seems more interesting and exciting down here. Nevada was just dead in comparison."

Next day they entered Arizona and that night slept in a "Rock Prairie . . . 80 Miles East of California." They picked up mail in Phoenix, "had Mike greased and gassed, and then left." Arizona was "not as interesting as . . . Texas. The roads are paved and the weather is plenty hot."

They were really covering the miles now, doing 190, 195, 150 miles a day, stopping as little as possible. Dib tried to write a letter in Mike while Tod drove but had to "stop as its hopeless." Past Yuma, "a lazy Spanish town," they "crossed the Colorado River into good ole California. We stopped and had our baggage, etc. looked at. The officers said O.K., so we continued over rolling sand dunes and desert. The roads are keen, brand new. Gas is 16¢ in Yuma so we filled up. . . . Earlier in the day Mike had stopped on us so we cleaned the carborator before turning in." It was October 31, Halloween.

At the Fort Yuma Inspection Station they were given a California State Agriculture certificate to "retain while in California." On the back it explained:

This inspection was made to intercept plants or plant products such as fruits, vegetables, cotton seed, etc., being carried into California in violation of State Plant Quarantine Regulations and which might be the means of introducing such serious agricultural pests as:

Cotton Boll Weevil, which did an estimated damage of $400,000,000 to the cotton crop of the United States last year. This insect does not exist in California.
Citrus Canker Disease, readily carried on oranges, grapefruit and other citrus fruits — occurs in the southern states where $20,000,000 has been expended or lost in attempting eradication. This disease does not occur in California.
Alfalfa Weevil, the most serious pest of alfalfa. Readily carried in bedding and other camping equipment. Thousands of these insects are removed each year from equip-

It was hard to pass up Tijuana, no matter how anxious they were to get home.
This postcard of the Bell Tower went to Gert and Helen.

ment inspected at border quarantine station.

They climbed the mountains approaching San Diego, with Mike getting "hot around the collar," and then felt that good ocean air again. They breezed through San Diego and headed for "Tia Juana" as their Rand McNally spelled it, to make camp "In Some Mexican's Field" outside the town. Dib wrote his last letter home and said, "Gee mom (& all), I wish you were with us. You ought to see Tia Juana, what a wide open place. Every store & stand has a bar. All kinds of drinks are served. How do I know? Well I saw them & read the sign boards. 'Old Judge Whiskey', 'A.B.C. Beer', 'Gray Fox.' You don't have to worry about us. . . . At the border they were stopping everyone before they entered Mex. They let us infants through. Tia Juana came shortly, & it impressed me as busy & wild. Of course today is Sun. tomorrow it may be dead." Tijuana, no doubt tamer

in 1931 than it may have been since, was still a wide-open border town where you could get easily married, divorced, drunk, or ahem. Apparently Dib and Tod were too broke to get into too much trouble. Dib wrote, "Lucky we are nearly broke or else we would taste some 'Gray Fox.'" He liked the name of what was apparently a local beer.

Next moring Mike was reluctant to get started, as they were on the coast in the fog and damp once again. After calling at the Mexican post office, they crossed back into the U.S., the officers making them take Mike apart for inspection. Once finished Dib recorded, "We got a good view of San Diego Harbor and City. We saw Lindbergh's Field."

Highways in southern California were as good as they had been back east. Outside San Diego they picked up U.S. 101, also called the Pacific Highway, which was the major road north. A secondary "improved" road ran directly along the water in some places but wasn't even given a num-

At the border you spread your things on a portable table and the custom officials did their work.
It looks like Mike is waiting to go through.

ber in the Rand McNally. On the other side of Los Angeles the road was not yet finished between Santa Monica and Oxnard.

"After passing through plenty small cities and towns we arrived in Los Angeles about 3:30 p.m." The small cities were La Jolla, Del Mar, Encinitas, Oceanside. "The highways are swell," two lanes as far as they could remember, and traffic was very light. In Hollywood they drove by Studio City and took a picture, but they were in too much of a homesick hurry to take a tour. For $1 they rented an auto camp for the night.

Next day they "got up 6 a.m. ate and had a good shower." They had an "awful time starting Mike and then he wouldn't pull any hills and was using too much gas, so we adjusted the timing and she ran O.K." They kept to Interstate 101 through Santa Monica, Ventura, Santa Barbara, Santa Maria, Pismo Beach, San Luis Obispo, stopping briefly to eat at 4:00 p.m. and then driving on into the night. They covered a record 275 miles in one day, indicating how anxious they were to get home, eventually settling in an or-

chard off the highway about 150 miles south of San Francisco to sleep.

In the morning, their larder pretty bare by now, they fried apples for breakfast. But if they were anxious to get on the highway, Mike wasn't. It took over an hour to crank the old Lizzie to a start. The night had been damp, foggy, and chilly, and the Ford had good reason to be difficult. Dib wrote his last entry November 4, 1931, "At last we got started and we traveled much faster than usual. We finally began to recognize familiar places. The sun is out warmer. We stopped in Palo Alto for milk shakes — our last 30¢. The signs all along the road tell us we're getting closer to home. Near Colma we hit the expected Frisco Fog. We got going plenty fast now."

When they got to 26th Avenue they stopped briefly at the Robinson's to give Pinky a hard time about his cast-off car and "then home with the whistle wide open. Got a tumble from Miss Klier (a young lady in the neighborhood). Hooray! ! A happy reunion. Hit the hay late and all are O.K."

Dib leans against Mike on a new hand-carved cane in front of John King's Place.
Notice the slot machines in the back, and the waterbags on the car.

Mike getting some "tumbles" on the streets of Tijuana.

In Hollywood, they stop just long enough to drive by a movie studio before heading home.

EPILOGUE

Farewell, My Lovely

(The Model T) was the miracle God had wrought. And it was patently the sort of thing that could only happen once. Mechanically uncanny, it was like nothing that had ever come to the world before. Flourishing industries rose and fell with it. As a vehicle, it was hard-working, commonplace, heroic; and it often seemed to transmit those qualities to the persons who rode in it.

— From the Lee Strout White (E.B. White and Richard L. Strout) book *Farewell to Model T*, 1936, G.P. Putnam's Sons

They had made it, across the U.S. of A. and back, despite a little minor carburetor and timing trouble toward the end of the journey, despite the mismated axle, a hole in the radiator, and a lot of old shoes wearing out on the way.

Not long after the trip, Dib and Tod raced Mike down the Coast Highway again with someone clocking, and the old flivver hit fifty miles an hour . . . despite those disputable 9,000 bumpy miles.

As for Dib and Tod, they had done the trip and lost their fascination for Mike. Tod's mother did forgive him. He got his job at the ink factory back and eventually moved to San Bruno and had his own gas station and garage. Dib did a variety of things for those lean years in the thirties and eventually wound up working for the city of San Francisco as a forester. Neither of them ever got back to Texas, and Dib never saw his Connecticut relatives again.

The trip had changed them in the way trips do, directing their thoughts beyond the narrow confines of their everyday lives, yet taking a backseat to everyday necessities once they returned. Yet they were never quite the same two young men who had left home to cross country in September, 1931. They had seen the United States from sea to sea, glimpsed the history of their time first hand, and would always somehow remember it in that vastness of space and time that made up a late summer of their youth, complete and confined to memory that colored all that they felt or saw ever after.

But in 1932, when they were twenty, they were both more interested in taking darby young girls on picnics than in traveling across the country in an old heap. Dib remembers, "I kept the Ford maybe a year after the trip, on the outside. I worked in a nursery at 31st and Geary, and I'd drive it there and back every week. It was getting a little shabby and we wanted something better for our girlfriends. I got a Chevrolet Landau Sedan with a folded back, very fancy. I think it was a 1926 model, used. I gave Mike to a fellow, Mack, who lived a block away from us. He was on WPA subsistence and couldn't find work."

Mack used Mike for a while until the radiator got damaged, and he decided to dismantle the engine to give to a friend who had a boat on Lake Tahoe. The chassis he carted to the dump outside San Francisco in Brisbane.

The dump was right alongside the highway, and for a little while, at least, every time they drove out that way on a picnic or joy ride in Dib's new Chevrolet or the spiffy '28 Ajax Roadster Tod had acquired with wooden sides and canvas top, they'd point at the Lizzie out in the corner of the lot. You could still see the stenciled letters on Mike's body.

But they were much more interested in the Chevrolet and Ajax and in going thirty to forty miles an hour instead of twenty or twenty-five, and pretty soon they were speeding too fast to see the old Lizzie anymore.

Mike, Dib, and his Mom shortly after the trip, in front of their home, 731 41st avenue, San Francisco.

Back home after a reported (but doubtful) 9,000 bumpy miles, Dib and Tod pose with their Model T, "Mike," and all their trophies for a San Francisco newspaper photo. Notice all the states painted on the back of the cab, and the steer's head from the Texas desert attached to the well-worn spare tires.

Yvonne Ellingson is a freelance writer from Mill Valley, California who has crossed the continent several times by car, but never in an auto as picturesque as Mike. She worked in advertising, as a copywriter, and spent two years in Rome working as a journalist. From *Sea to Sea in a Model T* is her first book.

Left to right: Tod Snedeker (now deceased), Yvonne Ellingson, and Brian (Dib) Fewer.

2/01 (Π) 7/10 RA

F
UNITE

INDEX TO NATIONAL PARKS AND NATIONAL MONUMENTS

1 ANTIETAM BATTLE FIELD N. P.	D-11	35 MESA VERDE N. P.	E-4
2 AZTEC RUIN N. M.	E-4	36 MONTEZUMA CASTLE N. M.	F-3
3 BANDELIER N. M.	E-4	37 MOUND CITY GROUP N. M.	D-1
4 BIG HOLE BATTLE FIELD N. M.	C-3	38 MT. OLYMPUS N. M.	A-1
5 BRYCE CANYON N. M.	E-3	39 MUIR WOODS N. M.	D-1
6 CABRILLO N. M.	F-2	40 NATIONAL BISON RANCH N. M.	B-3
7 CAPULIN MOUNTAIN N. M.	E-5	41 NATURAL BRIDGES N. M.	E-3
8 CARLSBAD CAVE N. M.	G-5	42 NAVAJO N. M.	E-1
9 CASA GRANDE N. M.	F-3	43 OREGON CAVES N. M.	D-2
10 CHACO CANYON N. M.	E-4	44 PAPAGO SAGUARO N. M.	F-3
11 CHICKAMAUGA & CHATTANOOGA N. P.	F-9	45 PETRIFIED FOREST N. M.	F-3
12 CHIRICAHUA N. M.	F-3	46 PINNACLES N. M.	D-2
13 COLORADO N. M.	D-4	47 PIPE SPRING N. M.	E-3
14 CRATERS OF THE MOON N. M.	C-3	48 PLATT N. P.	F-6
15 CUSTER BATTLE FIELD	C-4	49 PT. PELEE N. P.	C-9
16 DEVIL POSTPILE N. M.	D-2	50 RAINBOW BRIDGE N. M.	E-3
17 DEVILS TOWER N. M.	C-5	51 ROCKY MOUNTAIN N. P.	D-4
18 DINOSAUR N. M.	D-4	52 SCOTTS BLUFF N. M.	D-4
19 EL MORRO N. M.	F-4	53 SEQUOIA N. P.	E-2
20 FOSSIL CYCAD N. M.	C-5	54 SHENANDOAH N. P.	D-2
21 GENERAL GRANT N. P.	E-2	55 SHILOH N. P.	F-8
22 GETTYSBURG N. P.	D-11	56 SHOSHONE CAVERN N. M.	C-4
23 GILA CLIFF DWELLINGS N. M.	F-4	57 SULLYS HILL N. P.	B-5
24 GRAN QUIVIRA N. M.	F-4	58 TIMPANOGOS CAVE N. M.	D-3
25 GREAT SMOKY MTS. N. P.	E-10	59 TONTO N. M.	F-3
26 GUILFORD COURTHOUSE N. P.	E-10	60 TUMACACORI N. M.	F-3
27 HOT SPRINGS N. P.	F-7	61 VERENDRYE N. M.	B-4
28 HOVENWEEP N. M.	E-4	62 VICKSBURG N. P.	G-8
29 JEWEL CAVE N. M.	C-5	63 WALNUT CANYON N. M.	C-4
30 LAFAYETTE N. P.	B-12	64 WHEELER N. M.	E-4
31 LASSEN VOLCANIC N. P.	C-1	65 WIND CAVE N. P.	C-5
32 LEHMAN CAVES N. M.	D-3	66 YUCCA HOUSE N. M.	E-4
33 LEWIS & CLARK CAVERN N. M.	B-3	67 ZION N. M.	E-3
34 LINCOLN BIRTHPLACE N. P.	E-9		

SCALE OF MILES

H-44

COPYRIGHT BY RAND McNALLY & CO. CHICAGO, ILL. MADE IN U.S.A.